PEOPLE LIKE US

PEOPLE LIKE US

The New Wave of Candidates Knocking at Democracy's Door

Sayu Bhojwani

THE
NEW
PRESS

NEW YORK
LONDON

Requests for permission to reproduce selections from this book should be mailed to:
Permissions Department, The New Press, 120 Wall Street, 31st floor, New York, NY
10005.

Published in the United States by The New Press, New York, 2018
Distributed by Two Rivers Distribution

ISBN 978-1-62097-414-8 (hc)
ISBN 978-1-62097-415-5 (ebook)
CIP data is available

The New Press publishes books that promote and enrich public discussion and
understanding of the issues vital to our democracy and to a more equitable world.
These books are made possible by the enthusiasm of our readers; the support of a
committed group of donors, large and small; the collaboration of our many partners
in the independent media and the not-for-profit sector; booksellers, who often hand-
sell New Press books; librarians; and above all by our authors.

www.thenewpress.com

Composition by Dix!
This book was set in Bembo

Printed in the United States of America

10 9 8 7 6 5 4 3 2 1

To my immigrant families

For democracy is never a final achievement.
It is a call to effort, to sacrifice . . .
—John F. Kennedy, 1963

America at its best is a place where people from
a multitude of backgrounds work together to safeguard
the rights and enrich the lives of all.
—Madeleine Albright, 2018

CONTENTS

INTRODUCTION

The founding fathers may have envisioned a representative democracy "by the people, for the people, and of the people," but the *people like us* after whom this book is named are not who these early leaders had in mind. By our founders' standards, American democracy is working as planned, serving the needs of the wealthy and well-connected. But by everyone else's standards, American democracy is broken. Those elected to represent us regularly fail to fight for our interests because they often do not reflect the country's demographics or breadth of experiences. To correct this course, we must foster a democracy that is built on our country's original ideals of freedom and justice, one that is more inclusive and representative of *people like us.*

When we look at demographics in the United States, visit schools and workplaces, or attend religious services, we see an incredibly diverse America. Whites are 63 percent of the country's population, Latinx 16 percent, African Americans 13 percent, and Asian Americans 5 percent; the other 3 percent identify as mixed race or other.[1] The top five countries that immigrants come from are Mexico, India, the Philippines, China, and Vietnam, in that order.[2] By the time the 2020 census takes place, more than half of all American children will belong to a racial minority group.[3] Despite this increasing diversity, Congress still looks like it did in the distant past: its members are 81 percent white and male, and only 7.1 percent are women of color.[4] Although the 115th Congress is the most diverse in history, only 9.4 percent of its members are African American, 8.5 percent Latinx, and 3.3 percent Asian Americans.[5]

Beyond Congress, the numbers are not much better. White men currently make up only 31 percent of the population but hold 65 percent of the elected positions in state and local governments.[6] Latinx and Asian Americans are the fastest-growing immigrant groups but hold only 2 percent of the five hundred thousand local and state elected offices.[7] This representation gap—between who Americans are and who our leaders are—is not coincidental. Instead, it is an intentional product of history and systemic white supremacy.

Despite this gap, America's foundational vision remains inspiring, particularly to immigrants and refugees. Either new to democracy or newly positioned to engage in democratic institutions after they become citizens, they are particularly optimistic about our founding principles even when their experiences run counter to the ideals. Drawn to the promise of America, they have crossed sometimes arbitrary borders from the south and north, or journeyed across oceans to seek better opportunities.

This promise of America has helped make immigrants the key driver of population growth for the past fifty years and will do so for the next fifty.[8] One in four Americans today is an immigrant or a child of at least one immigrant parent.[9] In 2065, that ratio will grow to one in three. In addition, every year more than half a million new Americans gain citizenship.[10]

Long before the 2016 election, immigrants participated in public and political life. Even if they were not eligible voters, immigrants who belonged to unions engaged in protests and called elected officials; others, active members of community organizations, conducted voter registration drives, promoted voter education activities, led petition or ballot referendum drives, and testified at hearings in Congress, city councils, or school boards about the impact of policy. But the Trump administration's policies have injected immigrant communities with an unparalleled fervor for political action. The silver lining to this dramatic change in the Oval Office is that citizen activism by new Americans has grown, with more of them taking to the streets, challenging elected officials, and raising funds—in greater numbers and with more visibility. Young people, women of color, and immigrants have been at the forefront of every social movement of the last decade—and the early months of the Trump administration have made this trend even more pronounced.

In this book, I tell stories of these newly energized Americans: immigrants or refugees themselves, the children of immigrants and refugees, and those from long-standing immigrant communities who continue to be seen as outsiders or foreigners. I assert by these examples that new Americans are well positioned to lead the fight for a just democracy. They have struggled to get and stay here, navigating complex bureaucracies and long waits for formal citizenship. Some have crossed dangerous borders, risking their own or their children's lives. For others, the United States was their final destination following stays in refugee camps in one or more countries. Each of these journeys has involved struggle, aspects of which may be less familiar to some native-born Americans.

Just like America's founding fathers who fought for an America independent of Britain, these new Americans are the strongest champions of democracy. Their commitment to and enthusiasm for America is a highly underutilized resource, and in *People Like Us*, I offer ways to leverage this resource more effectively to transform and invigorate our democracy.

To do so requires addressing the systemic obstacles that make it difficult for people of color, immigrants, and women to seek out and secure elected positions. The most pervasive obstacles for newcomers include the influence of money in politics, the lack of term limits, discriminatory redistricting, political gatekeeping, and the high financial cost of public life. Navigating these obstacles requires luck and perseverance, as the stories in this book will show. By benefiting from public financing of some elections, running for office in newly drawn districts, doggedly pursuing office even without the blessing of gatekeepers, and juggling their roles in public office with part-time or consulting work, Americans from a wider range of diverse racial, ethnic, and religious backgrounds than ever before are getting elected to, and serving in, city councils and state legislatures.

For valid reasons, politics is associated with a high price tag, from the cost of running for office to corporate contributions designed to win influence. Most Americans—in fact, 66 percent—think money has too much influence on campaigns, and this is not just conjecture.[11] More money is spent on campaigns than ever before, and not just on presidential and congressional races. From 2000 to 2016, contributions to state house races across the country nearly doubled, from $398 million in 2000, to $726 million in 2016.[12] State senate contributions saw the same level of growth, from $240 million in 2000, to $437 million in 2016.[13]

Not all of these contributions can be attributed easily to an individual or organization. The *Citizens United* decision by the U.S. Supreme Court in 2010 ruled that political spending is a form of protected speech under the First Amendment, and the government may not keep corporations or unions from spending money to support or denounce individual candidates in elections, allowing for unrestricted spending by corporations and other organized entities. Corporations have taken advantage of this relatively new policy, giving unlimited—and often difficult to trace—donations to certain candidates, tacitly encouraging them to support policies that are favorable to corporate interests, potentially at the expense of their constituents. Unions and nonprofit groups with competing interests could now support different candidates and vie to outspend each other in an effort to help their candidates, without the candidates' knowledge. This type of "uncoordinated" expenditure has grown on both sides of the aisle since 2010.

This growth has helped to increase the influence of "dark money," which refers to contributions that don't need to be reported, are untraceable to their source, and are used to influence the outcome of an election.[14] Also on the rise is the use of "gray money," which the Brennan Center for Justice (a law and public policy institute) defines as money that is reported by state super PACs (political action committees) but can come from sources that are not clearly traceable because of a lack of transparency.[15] Put together, gray and dark monies obscure the actual costs of a campaign by adding resources that can't clearly be measured.

As campaign contributions have become larger and more difficult to trace, new programs to help reduce the effect of money on politics have emerged. Public financing, or the use of tax dollars to support political campaigns, can be achieved by directing contributions from the state, such as is done in Arizona, where the Clean Elections Law helped Athena Salman and Isela Blanc run for and win their seats as representatives of District 26 in Arizona's state legislature. Another way that public financing can work is through matching dollars, as has been implemented in New York City, where candidates for the city council receive a 6:1 match for every dollar they raise. Carlos Menchaca, the city's first Mexican American council member, won his first race in 2013 in part because the match gave him access to more money than he would have been able to raise alone. This kind of campaign support from public sources provides political newcomers with a more level playing field.

But money matters much earlier in the process too, weighing heavily on a candidate's decision to run for office in the first place. Given the low salaries that most legislators earn, candidates for office have to consider whether or not they can afford to pursue a life of public service. State legislators like Athena and Isela in Arizona earn $24,000 a year, and, in Georgia, Sam Park, who was elected to the Georgia State Assembly in 2016, earns $17,342 annually.[16] Although these jobs are part-time in theory, they actually require full-time commitments. Balancing the life and responsibilities of a legislator alongside those of any second job would be a challenge for most people, and legislators struggle to do so in order to pay their bills. Many Americans don't even consider running because of these financial concerns—leaving the country's legislative bodies in the hands of wealthier individuals who are less likely to understand the concerns of constituents who come from diverse class backgrounds.

Discriminatory redistricting and a lack of term limits can serve as barriers to entry for political newcomers, just as much as financial concerns do. Redistricting most commonly comes up in the context of gerrymandering, the often-unfair process by which the lines of a district are drawn to benefit one group or political party over another. Gerrymandering can result in districts that look like amoebas and sometimes split communities in illogical ways, such as in the middle of a block.[17] Though it is most often discussed in the context of the two-party system, redistricting can also help determine how a district is drawn to benefit "communities of interest," or groups unified by race, class, culture, or other "interest."[18] Redistricting's primary purpose should be to ensure the adequate distribution of political power, a purpose that sometimes gets lost in the heat of the debate. In advance of the decennial U.S. census, which helps to determine whether states will gain or lose congressional seats, the discussion of how districts will be drawn, created, or eliminated becomes increasingly prominent.

A lesser-known aspect of redistricting that can benefit groups who lack adequate representation has been used in local elections, which can be at-large or district-based. At-large elections, in which all the residents of a city, school district, or other local entity elect representatives to the body that represents them, tend to favor candidates who have more resources and connections, since the candidates need to be recognized and reach voters across larger geographic areas. Districts—sometimes called wards—are smaller units within a city, school district, or other local entity. When an election is district-based, candidates only need to reach voters in their districts and to be known there in order to win a seat. Also called single-member districts, they are advantageous to political newcomers because the newcomers can start small, both in terms of the money they require and the voters they need to reach. A 2001 study by the National League of Cities, an organization that serves as a resource and advocate for America's cities and municipal leaders, found that 16 percent of America's large cities (defined as those with a population greater than 200,000) had at-large elections. Ethnic or racial groups who are living only in some areas of those cities are thus at a disadvantage in electing someone from their own racial group or geographic area.[19]

Following the 2010 census, cities across the United States have made shifts to single-member districts as a result of citizen activism or legal action by residents and organizations seeking to achieve better representation of racial minority groups. In Detroit, Michigan, in 2013, Raquel Castañeda-López became the first Latina on the Detroit City Council, after the city moved from at-large to district-based elections. Carmen Méndez was one of three Latinas elected to the Yakima (Washington) City Council in 2015, making history as the first among three Latinas to serve in a city that is 43 percent Latinx. Anaheim and Garden Grove, two cities in Orange County, California (a majority-minority county in which only 44 percent of the population is white), now have district elections, and additional cities in the county are making the same change. These shifts in the way elections are run are helping to address the gap in representation of racial and ethnic minorities, but they are often laborious and contentious. When in place, however, they open doors that are otherwise difficult for newcomers to enter.

Term limits, which determine how long and for how many terms a legislator can hold office, give newcomers an opportunity to run for office. But currently only fifteen states limit how long their legislators can serve, according to a 2015 study by the National Council on State Legislatures.[20] In the other thirty-five states, candidates like Ilhan Omar, who won a seat on the Minnesota State Legislature, and Sam Park, who was elected to Georgia's state assembly in 2016, must defeat incumbents. Some argue that term limits reduce the number of experienced legislators and that voters can be the determinants of whether someone is popular enough to stay in office.[21] But long-serving legislators are not always well equipped to serve a district's changing population and can become accountable to special interests, instead of to their constituents. Assuming they will have power indefinitely, they can become less responsive to those who elected them in the first place. In general, sitting legislators, some of whom have been in office for decades, are reluctant to give up their perches of power, to usher in new voices who reflect the changing demographics of a district, and to bring renewed energy and diverse experiences to policymaking.

Both term limits and district-based elections create opportunities for a more representative democracy by ensuring that voters are able to choose from and elect someone who reflects who they are—whether that's Latinx, African immigrant, working-class, transgender, or millennial. Without fixing this aspect of democracy, we risk having leaders who are out of touch with the needs and experiences of their district's current residents and are thus unlikely to represent those experiences in their governance.

The founding fathers may have planned for a system that is more accessible to wealthy and well-connected men, but they likely didn't envision the ecosystem of political parties, unions, and issue-based organizations that would grow up around them. Leaders within the political party structure, senior union leaders, and the heads of major endorsing organizations that focus on particular issues have become powerful gatekeepers. In these roles, they determine who stays in—and who stays out of—the political arena.

Gatekeepers have multiple motives in selecting who will get support and who will not. When choosing between a new candidate who is just beginning to understand the political landscape and an incumbent with whom they have worked for some time, gatekeepers are invested in keeping power where it has been, with someone who is already familiar. The habit of gravitating to the familiar might extend beyond favoring an incumbent to favoring someone whom the gatekeepers know personally or to someone who looks like they do. When it comes to established political, union, and organization leadership that is predominantly white and male, "familiar" may also mean white and male.

Gatekeepers matter, because they can help catapult a candidate from being a relatively unknown name to being a household one, can bring financial contributions that boost a candidate's own fundraising capacity, and can provide support to reach voters through mailers and field outreach. Whether they are backing incumbents or new candidates, progressive and conservative gatekeepers preserve their interests by recruiting and supporting people whose views they are familiar with and whose votes they can rely on. In the 2016 California state house races, for example, $41 million in contributions to candidates came from the state's Democratic or Republican parties and from a range of unions, including those organizing the building trades, teachers, and service employees.[22]

On its face, this may seem logical, but the process of deciding who gets support tends to be an exclusive one, relying primarily on existing networks rather than on seeking out new voices or relationships. Such "gatekeeping" preserves power among those with access or those willing to make trade-offs in order to gain financial support and endorsements. Newcomers to the political process and to the United States are less likely to have relationships or commonalities with established gatekeepers in their communities, making it easier for the pattern of electing people who are well connected and well established to repeat itself.

Relying on existing networks and relationships is also not a strategic plan for building a leadership pipeline. Conservatives have been far more successful than progressives at recruiting and training candidates for all levels of office, from school boards to state legislatures. The Leadership Institute, a nonprofit that provides campaign training to conservatives, was started in 1979, and the Young America's Foundation, which helps develop conservative leaders on campuses across the country, was founded in 1998. After the 2016 election, a bevy of new organizations began recruiting and training progressive candidates, and thousands have signed up to run. But it remains unclear whether progressive organizations, including the Democratic Party, will stand behind people who literally and figuratively speak to a new America, or if they will double down on establishment candidates. More intentional recruitment and support will only occur when progressives are willing to accept that demographics are not destiny and to face their own implicit bias toward the familiar—that is white and male. Building a bench will be most strategic and effective when it is done with a lens that reflects the current and future reality of a multiracial America.

Immigrant candidates appeal to their burgeoning ethnic communities because of their shared experience, appearance, ethnicity, and values. As outsiders and newcomers, they also appeal to the large universe of voters who are demanding alternatives to current incumbents. They bring new strategies to campaigning that can expand the electorate and increase voter participation. Finally, they bring new voices to policymaking.

As Americans seek to reorient our democracy to be more just, accessible, and reflective, new Americans will play a critical role. Eligible voters in this country are increasingly diverse. Between the 2012 and 2016 elections, the numbers of Asian American and Latinx voters grew by 16 percent and 17 percent, respectively.[23] The growth in Latinx and Asian American voters in battleground states means that even small increases in their turnout can affect the outcome of elections. In 2016, Lan Diep, the eldest son of political refugees from Vietnam, won a seat on the San Jose City Council by just 12 votes. In Arizona, Latinx now make up 22 percent of eligible voters, 18 percent of them in Florida, and 17 percent in Nevada. Asian Americans make up more than 5 percent of the eligible voters in Nevada and Virginia. These statistics matter for presidential elections but even more for down-ballot races, in which a handful of votes can determine the winner.

Because these candidates reflect the experiences of their voters—through their immigration stories, economic experiences, and social conditions—they understand what it means to be outside of traditional political circles. Rather than seeing that as a deterrent, new American candidates can leverage their status as outsiders to identify and connect with new and low-propensity voters.

In the following pages, I show how new American

candidates are able to transcend class and ethnicity to appeal to a broad cross section of voters. They can connect with working-class people of all backgrounds, with whom they often share similar economic struggles. For liberal whites, immigrant candidates reinforce a vision of America that is inclusive and opportunity-filled. In places like Minneapolis and Detroit, immigrants have built successful political coalitions that include white voters and voters of color, demonstrating the broad appeal of immigrant voices.

Once they're in office, these policymakers bring their voices to the conversation, shaping the discussion about educational equity, for instance, by articulating the particular challenges faced by mixed-status families that include undocumented parents and American-born children. How do non-English-dominant parents who fear for their immigration status interact with schools, for example? Conversations about democratic reforms such as automatic voter registration might benefit from the experience of a policymaker who is a naturalized citizen and who came to electoral politics because she first registered to vote when a nonprofit sought her out. How could direct voter contact continue to be a priority even if voters were automatically registered at the time they applied for driver's licenses?

Engaging new voters and contributing to the policy conversation are key strategies that immigrant candidates employ to strengthen American democracy and ensure that the progressive movement continues to be fueled by new voices and vantage points.

These contributions can reshape our institutions and our

outlook and build a stronger democracy, a more vibrant economy, and a more varied civic life. They can create the kind of democracy that Jose Moreno envisioned when he served as a plaintiff in a lawsuit against the City of Anaheim. At the time of the filing, the city's population was 53 percent Latinx, but not one Latinx was serving on the city council. Fixing that discrepancy became Jose's mission. Today, he serves on the Anaheim City Council, representing families and children whose experiences mirror his own as a once-undocumented immigrant from Mexico.

Jose's determination and commitment to the ideals of American democracy is no anomaly. He stands alongside millions of other immigrants whose optimism continues unabated in spite of an all-too-common exclusionary reality. That positive outlook is rooted in possibility, the possibility of serving in public office in a city where you were undocumented as a child, the possibility of defeating an incumbent who was elected to office before you were born, the possibility of getting elected without having to raise thousands of dollars.

Today, people who fulfill these possibilities are largely exceptions to the rule, rare people who overcome systemic and social obstacles to become the leaders we had been waiting for. But if we address the systemic barriers that have kept people like us out, American democracy can finally live up to its promise.

1

REDRAWING THE LINES OF POWER

Raquel Castañeda-López, the council member for Detroit's District 6, still wakes up in her childhood home with three of her sisters, her niece, and her brother. Her mother lives close enough to be a frequent presence and an occasional critic. In the eyes of her district's residents, Raquel serves as a powerful presence and advocate, but at home she is a sister, aunt, or daughter who is expected to pull her own weight in the extended family.

Born in Michigan, Raquel is a Mexican American. She runs marathons, lifts weights, and preplans her meals by freezing fruits and vegetables on the weekends. You're as likely to see her walking through City Hall in a suit jacket over a dress as you are to see her in jeans, sandals, and a T-shirt. She can seem unassuming and quiet—until she starts talking about her constituents' needs.

The district she represents is home to just over 100,000 residents, and includes part of Detroit's gentrifying downtown as well as the two zip codes with the highest number of Latinx in the city. Latinx and African Americans are each 39 percent of her constituency. Thirty-eight percent of the city's households have incomes below the poverty line, but the district is also home to hipsters running trendy bars, Syrian immigrants, and white trustafarians making artisanal bourbon. Afflicted by the automobile industry's decline, economic crises, and corruption, but now experiencing a boom in outsider interest and investment, the Motor City is both America's past and its future. Existing and emerging socioeconomic and ethnic realities are in almost constant conflict.

A political neophyte, Raquel was an unlikely candidate for this role. She was neither well connected to Detroit's political establishment nor well positioned with unions or business leaders. Despite lacking these connections, which often help situate candidates for political office, she was successful in her first run for city council in 2013. And she's not alone. From the urban Midwest to rural northeastern villages and southern border towns, local elections are becoming crucibles of change. The characteristics of each of these elections vary by region, but they share one commonality: they provide a pathway for newcomers interested in politics to run and win.

Even as presidential and congressional elections have become media and money magnets, many local elections remain accessible to emerging leaders. For newcomers seeking political power for the first time, local races are a critical entry point that allows them to serve their communities immediately and build a career trajectory that could lead to higher office. Each victory matters, since Asian Americans and Latinx—the two fastest-growing immigrant groups—hold only two percent of the country's more than five hundred thousand state and local offices. But because of several factors that have emerged since 2010, political glass ceilings are shattering in many cities. One of these factors is the redrawing of district lines, which has helped people like Raquel become one of many elected "firsts." In Detroit, Raquel benefited from a political moment effected in 2012: city council members, previously voted on by all city residents, would thereafter be elected from seven districts.

This change was set in motion before the 2010 census was taken, but data that emerges from a census often does result in a reexamination of the country's legislative districts. Following the census, the country's congressional districts are re-evaluated using the new population data. Each state, regardless of its population size, sends two representatives to the U.S. Senate. For the House of Representatives, however, the 435 seats are distributed to states according to an average number. In 2000, the average congressional district had a population of 647,000. In 2010, district sizes increased to 711,000.[1] To accommodate that change, some states lost seats, while others gained them. New York lost two, and in the process of creating new districts to redistribute the population from seats that were lost, the legislature took into account one of the state's most dramatic demographic changes: a 45 percent increase in its Asian American population.[2] Consequently, the newly drawn Congressional District 6 of New York included a population that was 38 percent Asian American.[3] Those demographics helped elect the state's first-ever Asian American representative, Congresswoman Grace Meng.

Washington's 9th congressional district, redrawn after the state gained a seat in Congress in 2010, became the state's first majority-minority district, which means that more of its residents are racial or ethnic minorities than are non-Hispanic whites.[4] The United States currently has 123 majority-minority districts, which represent 28 percent of the 435 House districts.[5] Some of these districts have a plurality of only one racial minority, meaning that the people of color in the district all belong to one racial minority group as defined by the Census Bureau. For example, California has a majority Asian American district, Texas has one that is majority Latinx, and Florida has one that is majority African American.[6]

At the same time that districts were being redrawn for Congress, cities large and small across the country began to reimagine what representation could look like in order to better reflect their residents. Citizens inside and outside of government led efforts to create more opportunities for diverse legislatures, such as the effort that was undertaken in Detroit. In 2009, voters there helped pass a referendum to move the city from at-large elections to district elections, or single-member districts. At-large elections require voters citywide to choose their representatives, whereas district elections allow voters to select a single candidate from their district to represent them in a multi-member legislative body such as a city council or school board. Because candidates just need to campaign and get support from a subsection of a city rather than from the whole city, district elections make it easier for candidates with strong community ties to be elected than at-large systems do. Most cities with at-large elections that have made the shift to district elections have done so because a racial or ethnic minority group that is a significant portion of the city's population has not had representation on the city council or school board; new districts are usually drawn to ensure that these groups are able to elect one of their own in one or more areas of the city.

In Detroit, single-member districts were expected to bring more ethnic and economic diversity to the council and increase the likelihood that residents could elect someone from their neighborhood to represent them. Despite the fact that voters adopted the referendum in 2009, politically motivated challenges filled the following years, largely filed by incumbent council members who feared that the change would increase their chances of being voted out of office. In 2012, the city's charter was finally revised to mandate new single-member districts. The city council drew the new maps for seven districts, with approximately 100,000 residents each, and the first elections for these seats took place in 2013.

The emergence of these new districts ushered in a pool of candidates whose roots lay in distinct communities in Detroit. The candidates no longer needed a citywide reputation to run. Prior to redistricting, all the council members were African American. In fact, since the 1970s, all but two city council members had been African American. That composition changed slightly in 2013 when it came to include Raquel, the first and only Latina to be elected in the history of Detroit.

Her election was the culmination of concerted efforts on the part of community leaders. They considered the existence of newly drawn District 6 a viable opportunity to have their interests represented by a Latinx candidate—someone who would embody their experiences and diversity, and who shared their struggles. When the new district was announced in the spring of 2013, Raquel was working at the Center for Latino and Latin American Studies Center at Wayne State University, a large public research university in Detroit. Trained as a social worker, she helped design the curriculum for incoming first-year and upper-level students, taught a course to help with college and career success, and ensured that students had supportive services such as access to scholarships, peer mentorships, and academic advising.

Prior to working at Wayne State, she had been the campaign manager for Rashida Tlaib, who served two terms in the Michigan House of Representatives, from 2009 to 2014. (Rashida is running for Congress in 2018 to fill the seat vacated by Congressman John Conyers, who had served since 1965 and who resigned in 2017 due to sexual harassment claims.[7]) After Rashida won the Democratic primary in August 2008, Raquel volunteered on Barack Obama's 2008 presidential campaign, registering voters. She also volunteered for Representative Tlaib's re-election campaign in 2010 and for the 2012 campaign to re-elect President Obama.

Despite this experience with campaigns, Raquel was not actively considering a run herself. In fact, as the politics of determining new districts for the Detroit City Council were playing out, Raquel was focused on cultivating her home garden and on nurturing her entrepreneurial interests. She was taking a course on launching a small business from Allied Media Projects (AMP), a nonprofit dedicated to cultivating a more just and creative world through media strategies. A gelato truck was the front-runner among her business ideas. As it happens, two women associated with AMP were instrumental in conversations Raquel had about running for office.

Well respected by her students and civically engaged Detroiters, Raquel received requests that she run from a wide range of district and city residents once the districts were drawn. Among those who encouraged her were neighbors with whom she played soccer. As she weighed whether or not a run for office was the best way to make the difference she wanted to make in her community, her family members provided their two cents' worth. Her siblings joked that her "bossiness" primed her for the job. Her mother was more circumspect: "I can't believe you would consider abandoning your students," she told Raquel. Her mother's words hurt, though Raquel realized that they were rooted in her fear that Raquel would become the target of public attacks and that she wouldn't be able to secure the resources required for campaigning. Her niece, who was twelve at the time, articulated this latter problem more succinctly: "But we're poor. Can we do this?"

Raquel's decision to run for the city council seat was ultimately motivated by her desire to prove that someone like her—a woman of color on the cusp of escaping poverty—could successfully campaign and win office. Guerrilla campaigning made up for her lack of resources. Family members, students, and neighbors fluent in English and Spanish blanketed the neighborhoods in the district so they could share their excitement about what Raquel could do as a representative of their community on the council.

To run for office in the United States, candidates, including those running for president, have to collect signatures from residents in the district they hope to represent. The number varies, depending on the level of office and the location in which the candidate is running.

As Raquel was amassing enough signatures to file for her candidacy, she remained conflicted about running. When she took the signatures to the clerk's office, she reflexively asked for the form she would need to withdraw. Incredulous that Raquel might not run after the show of support she had received, the clerk admonished her with words Raquel has not forgotten: "This is not about you; this is about your community."

Though Raquel was certain she'd be able to perform the duties of a council member, she still harbored a deep sense of self-doubt. She thought of herself as a social worker, a profession not typically associated with political power. As someone who had grown up poor, she couldn't imagine herself as an elected official. She also had concerns about how she would be received as a Mexican American seeking public office in Detroit, a city commonly understood to be predominantly black.

Raquel's ambition to serve propelled her toward the initial steps of a campaign, but the pervasive insecurities and fears she felt about her political aspirations threatened to prevent her from going all-in. The emotional and psychological hurdles of running for office, daunting for anyone, are magnified for immigrants. Race and heritage serve as powerful deterrents, due to their fear that they will be uniquely targeted or attacked because of their backgrounds. Some of the anxiety Raquel felt at the clerk's office was related to the fact that she hadn't previously seen anyone like herself represented in local leadership.

She knew that she wanted to run, but she had no example of someone else like her to show that it could be done.

Raquel's first campaign was very much a family affair. Her sisters ran the campaign, her brother contributed money and manpower, and her mother, at first a reluctant observer, eventually provided food and moral support to the campaign staff. She also lent her voice to a robocall and took time off work to help Raquel on Election Day. Although the newly drawn District 6 was seen as a "Latinx" district because of the large number of Latinx living there, the campaign relied on a coalition strategy to engage not only Latinx voters but also African American and white voters. Raquel's 2013 victory was widely celebrated in the media because of the campaign's inclusive approach and its historic nature.

During her first term in the council, she was able to make progress on issues that mattered to her. For instance, on a March day in 2016 as an intermittent rain cloaked the city in gray, Raquel repeatedly rescheduled the meetings she was supposed to attend outside of the office, while she waited for the year's budget negotiations to resume. She was determined not to let any postponement deter her from her cause. The mayor's office has final control of the budget, but council members can request resources for their district or for citywide special programs. For two years, Raquel had been fighting for support to get translation and interpretation services, with no luck. But on that March day, she was optimistic. For the first time since her election, Detroit had a budget surplus, making her request more viable than it had been in the past. Still, Raquel was the only one of the nine council members who had made a request for appropriations. Others were reluctant to jump through the political hoops required to get money for new initiatives.

The morning after the budget hearings, over *chilaquiles* at a local Mexican restaurant where Raquel is a regular, she was triumphant. She had secured $400,000 for language-access services, the first time in the city's history that such funding had been made available. The win, like many such victories, was made possible by dint of political savvy and compromise. Access will include services not just for English-language learners, but also for people who are hearing impaired. Her office did extensive research and preparation to make the case for a human rights compliance officer and for a city contract with a virtual language line to assist the Office of Immigrant Affairs. Both enable the city's residents, who speak over 126 languages, to gain access to important services to which they are entitled.

Despite progress like this, Raquel's 2017 re-election campaign was grueling. She faced personal attacks that sought to discredit her. Elections for the Detroit City Council are nonpartisan, meaning candidates don't have to be affiliated with opposing political parties to compete, and the top two vote-getters move forward from the primary to the general election. In her re-election campaign, she won 59 percent of the vote in the August primary, and her closest opponent, Tyrone Carter, won 33 percent. A Democrat, Tyrone is an African American who served in the Wayne County Sheriff's Office as an executive lieutenant for twenty-five years. He had run against Raquel in 2013, and had also lost three other elections, two for county commissioner and one for state representative.

The period from the August 8 primary to the November 7 general election was vicious, as she and Tyrone competed to win the council seat. Negative campaigning is often personal, but when it involves a candidate's family, it can be particularly difficult to bear. One mailer from Tyrone's campaign included a picture of the home in which Raquel lives with her sisters and brother; it cited housing code violations. Constituents drove by the home as a result, and Fox News ran a story, online and on television, with the headline "Is Detroit Councilwoman's home part of city's blight problem?"[8] In the story, Raquel was forced to defend herself and her family, laying bare the intergenerational family struggle with poverty that had ultimately led to the housing code violations her opponent cited. Over one hundred years old, the home serves as a source of pride and continuity; it is the place where her grandmother raised her children and her mother raised Raquel and her siblings. Even though she had mentally prepared for the challenges of her re-election, Raquel never imagined her family home would become a campaign issue.

Across the country in Yakima, Washington, Carmen Méndez, like Raquel, was elected as a result of a city's shift from at-large to single-member district elections. Unlike Raquel, who benefited from a district with a Latinx base, Carmen represents a district that is 90 percent white. Born in Yakima and raised in Mexico, Carmen is strikingly tall, with fashionable short hair and a glamorous air. She speaks in a steady and controlled manner, reinforcing the strength of her conviction and determination.

Carmen is a single parent like her own mother was. Her tween daughter is both a motivator and a supporter. "She's the reason I do everything I do," Carmen says, "so that one day she will have a better opportunity."

After spending most of her childhood in Colima, Mexico, Carmen returned to Yakima for high school and college. She was the first person in her family to complete college, where she began a career in service by winning the race for student council president. Then, in 2015, Carmen became one of three Latinas elected to the Yakima City Council, along with Dulce Gutiérrez and Avina Gutiérrez (no relation).

As with Raquel, Carmen did not need citywide name recognition or large campaign coffers to be elected; she only had to mobilize voters in her newly drawn district. To do so, Carmen ran a robust grassroots campaign, knocking on doors for weeks at a time to win over voters. She encountered racism and sexism from the voters in her predominantly white district, but she also found that they had a fundamental desire for human connection and for having their concerns heard by someone who could address them.

"So many people shut the door in my face because of what I looked like and my last name," said Carmen. "Even in this day [and age], people are so afraid of change. It's crazy." Carmen ran against four other candidates, who were all white. She chose the design for her yard signs knowing her ethnicity could be a drawback. The signs were emblazoned with CARMEN in large font and MENDEZ in small print below. Despite the hostility she encountered, Carmen maintained a tenacious work ethic. "I walked so much and doorbelled so much. I attended every forum and community gathering, even if it was a place I wasn't completely welcomed."

One of the voters Carmen visited was eighty-nine-year-old Trixie Koch, a white woman who was active with the League of Women Voters, which promotes women's involvement in democracy. At their first meeting, Trixie said, "I wasn't going to vote for you because I didn't know who you were, but since you came to me, I will vote." Trixie also made a campaign contribution and, perhaps more significantly, wrote a letter to everyone in her neighborhood in support of Carmen. "She doorbelled with me when it was one hundred and two degrees. We had nothing in common—besides the fact that we agreed that our community needed change." Carmen beat her opponent by 9 percentage points, demonstrating that a candidate's ethnicity can be tangential to constituents' choices at the ballot box.

However, being Latina didn't mean Carmen or Raquel were warmly accepted by all of their constituents of color. After Carmen had assumed office, a fellow Latino asked her, "Are you just a coconut?"—a term often used derogatorily against people who are "brown-skinned" on the outside but "act white."

"I didn't understand what he was saying," Carmen recalled. "At times, I feel they [Latinos] are the ones who are the most critical about us. I am trying to walk this fine line that affirms I'm able to relate to the Anglo constituents but I can also relate to the Latino community."

Immigrants in elected office tread a perilous path. They represent all of their constituents, not just those with whom they share an ethnicity. Raquel describes her district as approximately 40 percent African American, 40 percent Latinx, and 20 percent white. But because of her advocacy on behalf of immigrant communities, Arab Americans—a few of whom live in her district and others who come from nearby Dearborn, which is home to the largest Arab American population in the country—frequent her office.

"My constituents asked how many African Americans I had on staff, or why I'm going to so many Latino events," Raquel said. "So, we started to keep track of the events." She added, "I also asked them if they were asking other council members the same questions."

Carmen and Raquel are poster children for the Latinx community, but they are also subject to greater levels of scrutiny and accountability by both fellow Latinx and other constituents. Carmen and Raquel are public servants, women of color, and Latinas. These identities shouldn't be at odds with one another, and often aren't, but ethnic identity is a visual marker that neither can escape. Neither feels completely accepted as the Americans or leaders that they are.

On the Yakima City Council, Carmen and the other two Latinas who were elected at the same time are occasionally mistaken for one another. For that reason, when official seating in the council chambers was being assigned, Carmen suggested they not sit next to each other. "We already get looked at as a whole versus being seen as individuals," she said. Two years after having begun her term, Carmen says she's still "mistaken" for her fellow councilmember Dulce Gutiérrez when she is out and about in Yakima. She has received campaign contributions addressed to Carmen Garcia and to Carmen Lopez, instead of to Carmen Méndez, a sign that even her supporters are capable of transforming her into a generic Latina identity.

Grappling with identity is not new to Carmen. As a child in Mexico, she was called "the American kid" by her classmates; back in Yakima, she was "the Mexican." But being reminded of her difference is still jarring, even when it comes from well-intentioned friends. One of those incidents occurred when Carmen first considered joining the council.

In 2013, Yakima council member Sara Bristol resigned because she and her family were relocating. When seeking her replacement, the council invited interested residents of District 2 to submit a short application that asked them the reasons for their interest and their potential qualifications for serving.[9] The council would select a replacement from the applicants, and that person would serve until the next election took place in November 2015. Carmen wanted to put her name up for consideration, but a white friend told her, "I'm going to be very frank with you. You will never get appointed to City Council because of your last name. Don't do it. It's going to be a waste of your time." Discouraged, she held back, but thirteen others, including two women, applied. Six finalists were interviewed, and Tom Dittmar, an investigator in the Yakima office of the state's Department of Labor and Industries was chosen to fill the vacancy, perhaps proving Carmen's friend right.

As the appointment process was unfolding, the Yakima City Council was also in the middle of a lawsuit. In 2012, the ACLU had sued the City of Yakima on behalf of two of its residents—Rogelio Montes, who had run unsuccessfully for the city council in 2011, and Mateo Ortega, a university administrator—who argued that the existing system of electing only at-large council members limited the potential of minorities to meaningfully influence the outcome of elections and was in violation of Section 2 of the federal Voting Rights Act.[10]

Yakima's population was then 40 percent Latinx, but in the council's thirty-seven-year history, the council had never had a Latinx representative. Since the ACLU's filing, the city's population has changed, and in 2017 its residents were 43 percent Latinx and 51 percent white.[11]

The ACLU won its lawsuit against Yakima in August 2014, and the judge asked for proposals from the City of Yakima and the ACLU for a new system that would support the election of Latinx. In February 2015, the judge approved the ACLU's plan, which proposed seven districts. Newly drawn Districts 1 and 2 were majority Latinx, and both districts elected a Latina in 2015: Dulce Gutiérrez to District 1, where she won 85 percent of the vote, and Avina Gutiérrez to District 2, where she won 69 percent of the vote.

The redistricting process allowed Carmen her first real opportunity to run for office, though she didn't live in a majority Latinx district. Her home of two years was in the newly drawn, predominately white District 3. Still, Carmen, determined and enthusiastic, was the first candidate to file her intention to run with the Yakima County Elections office. She went on to win by a margin of 160 votes in a district that was only 8 percent Latinx.[12]

Redistricting is one of many ways to ensure that new voices like Carmen's and Raquel's make it into government. The process of redrawing election-district boundaries has been fraught with controversy and slowed by legal battles in many of the places where it has been tried, particularly in recent decades. In particular, two practices—cracking and packing—are of great concern. Cracking refers to splitting voters of similar interests—partisan identity, race or ethnicity, or geographic proximity—into multiple districts to dilute the impact of their vote. Packing refers to densely concentrating similar voters into one district so that a candidate can win that one district with an overwhelming majority.

Public disgust with the redistricting process often stems from situations in which legislators draw the lines of their own districts in order to preserve the advantage they have with voters who know their names and track records, instead of ensuring that the district is an accurate reflection of a community that is united by race, class, or geographic proximity. The most high-profile case on this matter developed in Wisconsin. In 2011, Republican state legislators there drew maps that would ensure their ability to win seats in upcoming election cycles. Wisconsin Democrats sued the state in 2016, alleging that their votes were being "wasted" because of cracking and packing. In 2018, the Supreme Court dismissed the case, *Gill v. Whitford*, and sent it back to the district court for reargument, effectively punting a decision on partisan gerrymandering.

In local elections for school boards and city councils, for example, redistricting can manifest differently than it does in state-level elections like Wisconsin's. As was the case for Carmen and Raquel, redistricting created new opportunities for elected officials from underrepresented communities to secure seats at the table.

In a hypothetical city of 200,000 residents, where schoolteachers, firefighters, security guards, small-business owners, corporate executives, and tech entrepreneurs live and work, it's unlikely that a local teacher will be well known citywide. Nor is it likely that most of the city's residents will share the same concerns about education, public spaces, or economic development. If the city elects its council at-large, the candidates most likely to win are those who have name recognition citywide, or have the resources to buy advertisements, place yard signs, and send mailers to reach 200,000 residents—or at least the voters among them. On the other hand, with a district-based election—with, say, eight districts of 25,000 residents each—that local schoolteacher who's well known in her local community has to focus only on those 25,000 residents. She can rely on her strong local reputation, knock on doors in a small geographical area, show up only at local events, and generally spend—and thus need to raise—less money. In addition, local residents are more likely to feel connected to their elected representative if it's someone who lives and works in their community.

Because of the wealth gap among voters, in which voters are likely to be wealthier than non-voters, the participating voters to whom an at-large elected representative gives attention are also less likely to be from the city's low-income communities.[13] They are more likely to be listening to the concerns of voters in areas that are already well resourced. Since people in those areas feel more connected and responded to, they are more likely to continue voting regularly. This creates a vicious cycle, with a city council member winning every election based on votes by the same people to whom she is responding. She won't try to get new people to come to the polls on Election Day because she doesn't need to. This is why the shift from at-large to local district elections is so appealing. Raquel and Carmen are proof of how effective local district elections can be in bringing underrepresented groups into positions of power.

The transformative power of district-based elections is not going unnoticed by those concerned with holding on to power. The Project for Fair Representation is a nonprofit legal defense fund that describes itself as supporting "litigation that challenges racial and ethnic classifications and preferences in state and federal courts."[14] Led by the conservative legal strategist Edward Blum, the group has been active since 2005 in cases that challenge universities, local governments, and the federal government for applying laws or policies that appear to favor minority groups in university admissions or through redistricting. The group filed a lawsuit in California's federal court challenging the constitutionality of the state's Voting Rights Act on behalf of Don Higginson, the former mayor of the city of Poway in San Diego County. The suit contends that recent decisions by localities in California to switch from at-large to district elections are making "race the only factor in redistricting."[15]

Individuals are at the heart of redistricting efforts to create more opportunities for racial and ethnic minorities to run and win elections. Yakima residents Rogelio and Mateo, the plaintiffs in the ACLU lawsuit against the city council, were frustrated by the fact that no one with a Latino surname had ever been elected to the council. Community organizer Jonathan Paik had similar concerns about Fullerton, California, and advocated on behalf of the city's Asian American communities for a change in the way representatives were elected there. Nearly one in four Fullerton residents is Asian American, and yet, in an echo of the situation in Yakima, no Asian American had ever served on its city council. Regular residents can become unmotivated to engage politically if they observe unfairness when it comes to representation from their ethnic community. Lawsuits like those filed in Yakima and Fullerton address representation via a lens that the average citizen might not use. But once resolved, they not only help ensure that elected officials more accurately represent their communities, they can also bring additional benefits such as programs to support and integrate communities who have been ignored or marginalized.

For example, with the settlement between the Yakima City Council and the ACLU came a requirement that the city invest $100,000 in programs to serve communities of color. Any programs had to be approved by the ACLU. One of the investments has been a mentoring program in which council members are assigned a high-school senior as a mentee. Students are expected to attend three council meetings and two committee meetings during the two-month period of the mentorship. Upon completion of their requirements, students receive a two-month paid internship at the city council, funded by dollars from the settlement.

In 2017, Carmen's mentee turned out to be her neighbor, a young woman who, like Carmen, was the first person in her family to go to college. Only the Latinas on the council supported their mentees in fulfilling their requirements, which meant that only those three students went on to received paid mentorships. Paying it forward is one way the councilwomen have had an impact.

Since 2016, the Latina councilwomen have also ensured that Spanish-language interpretation is available at council meetings. Following the 2016 elections, the council's chambers have been filled at every meeting with newly engaged Latinx and white constituents. Carmen indicates that the renewed interest comes from people who are concerned on both sides of the immigration issue; those who worry about the anti-immigrant climate for themselves or their Latinx neighbors, or both; and those who agree with the Trump administration's xenophobic and racist views.

But the push for district-based elections is not just about ethnicity. In another California city, Anaheim, the city council had elected Latinx members, but every single member had been elected from just one area of the city, its most affluent. Jose Moreno served as plaintiff in a lawsuit similar to the one filed in Yakima, challenging the Anaheim City Council. Following the lawsuit, Anaheim's resulting redistricting process was designed to create opportunities for representatives from more economically diverse sections of the city to be elected. For Jose and hundreds of others, a shift from at-large to district elections significantly lowers the barriers to entry and opens up opportunities for the election of representatives from historically underrepresented communities.

Carmen and Raquel benefited from redistricting and the political momentum it created in their communities. They answered a call to service and won their elections because of their determination and dedication. But they were also elected because of the hunger that Americans around the country have for new voices in government, regardless of ethnicity. Neither woman was elected solely because she is Latina, or by virtue of just the Latinx vote, given the demographics of their respective districts.

Gender and ethnicity were factors in their campaign, just as they are factors in their legislative activities. But voters elected them because they saw in them the promise and potential that they would deliver the kind of government the country is longing for. They are firsts, but they will need to be followed by many more. Not only will the advent of others like them close the representation gap between who Americans are and who American leaders are, but the power of expanding numbers will help cushion the impact of isolation and personal attacks that new American leaders experience. Carmen and Raquel find themselves in two worlds, one that is public and throbbing with opportunities for the exercise of power, and one that is private and rooted in humble beginnings, and over which linger the effects of insecurity and doubt.

Since Trump's election, Carmen has received emails that question her ability to serve, asking, "Are you legal? Are you even allowed to be on Council?" Other women also attack her for her appearance, with statements like "Stop playing dress-up and get to work." She describes these encounters as being discouraging initially but ultimately motivating.

"There's always going to be an issue," she says. "*We* are the issue, because we have power, and we're raising issues that affect our community."

Raquel shared a similar sentiment when reflecting on her 2017 re-election campaign. "I'm a brown, short woman who is educated, unmarried, and still lives in her ghetto childhood house, *and* I'm elected. My *existence* causes trouble."

The councilwomen's sentiments reflect the complex reality facing the United States as it seeks to be a more representative democracy. When some acquire power, others feel they are losing it. When the very people who have been objects of economic exploitation and racism become the subjects who have power and can wield it on behalf of their communities, the ground begins to shake beneath everyone. But this discomfort is unavoidable and necessary, for the transition from leaders who are disconnected from the realities of their constituents to those whose life experiences better position them to make policy that reflects those voters' concerns.

2

WAITING YOUR TURN

Ten years before Ilhan Omar was born in Somalia, Phyllis Kahn, a Jewish American Democrat from Brooklyn, New York, was elected to the Minnesota State Legislature. Kahn served for forty-four years until Ilhan unseated her in 2016 in a closely watched, politically heated, and widely celebrated race. Since her election, Ilhan has become a poster child for a new America: black, Muslim, and female. She appeared on the cover of *Time* magazine in September 2017 and is the subject of the documentary *Time for Ilhan*, by Flying Pieces Productions.

How did someone like Ilhan find her way into one of the most embattled races in Minnesota's recent history? Not overnight, and not without a fight.

Ilhan is tiny, with delicate features that are crowned by a head covering, often white, that adds several inches to her petite frame. Her smile is warm and generous but somehow still subdued. An ethnic Somali, she moved to Minneapolis at the age of fourteen, after her family had lived in a refugee camp in Kenya for four years. Her first years in America were spent in middle school, as a refugee. "I felt all of my otherness, as a black woman, Muslim, immigrant," she says.

But just over a year later, all that felt "suspended" when she received a certificate of student achievement signed by then president Bill Clinton. That moment was pivotal: it marked the first time she felt American. Even with all the public identities that seemed to marginalize her, she says, "To our president, I was just a student."

Millions of immigrants have stories like this one, about the moment when something shifts internally, moving them from asking, "What am I doing here?" to a moment like the one Ilhan had when she held that certificate in her hands and realized she could be just another American student. "I thought, I'm home; I'm fine."

As she adjusted to life in America, Ilhan also underwent a political journey at the side of her maternal grandfather, who was born in Somalia. Having grown up in a dictatorship, he was particularly excited about the possibility of having a voice in a representative democracy. She fondly remembers translating into Somali for him when he attended political party caucuses in Minnesota, and being influenced by his optimism about democracy. That early exposure to his ideas informed her later decision to major in political science and international studies at North Dakota State University.

Following college, her political experience included serving as senior policy aide in the office of Minneapolis City Council member Andrew Johnson, managing campaigns for local candidates, and being active in local party politics. In some ways, her path is typical: she had access to and experience with the political system before she ran. But her story remains an unlikely one because of her ability to defeat a longterm incumbent despite being a relative newcomer. Many acknowledge that Ilhan had long demonstrated rare leadership qualities. At the Women Organizing Women Network, a nonprofit based in Minneapolis whose goal is to empower first- and second-generation women to become civic and community leaders, one of Ilhan's coworkers, Habon Abdulle, saw something in her. Despite her demonstrated leadership, Habon says it took a full eight years to convince Ilhan to run.[1]

Ilhan says that moment came in November 2015, when she realized she could help secure better representation for her community and decided to challenge Representative Kahn for Minnesota's House District 60B. Of the district's approximately 39,000 residents, just over 4,000, or about 10 percent, were born in a country in Africa. Twenty percent of the district's residents self-report their ancestry as African, Ethiopian, or sub-Saharan African, one way to approximate the composition of the district since the census doesn't have a separate category for black immigrants.[2]

Ilhan's appeal extended to the entire district, but her political base included Minnesota's Somali community, which grew in the 1990s as Somali refugees fled from that country's civil war. Approximately 150,000 Somalis live in the United States, and 75,000 of them reside in Minnesota.[3] Many have settled in the Cedar-Riverside neighborhood, which was originally settled by Scandinavian immigrants in the 1890s. In the 1960s and 1970s, it became a more bohemian area, as hippies, artists, and intellectuals moved in. Soon thereafter, the area drew immigrants from Asia, Africa, and Latin America. From 1980 to 2010, the white population decreased from 82 percent to 39 percent. By 2010, 41 percent of Cedar-Riverside's residents reported their ancestry as sub-Saharan African or African.[4]

This diversity mattered, but Ilhan's campaign transcended basic identity politics, which can be so narrow as to focus exclusively on one ethnic group or issue. She describes cultivating all the subgroups in her district, from activists in the Black Lives Matter movement to established white progressives, from other young people of color to the East African media entities that African immigrants relied on. The Somali community was part of her winning coalition, but gaining their support was made more challenging because Mohamud Noor, a fellow Somali American in his late thirties, was also in the race. Mohamud, a computer scientist by training, had run for and lost races for the school board and state senate before challenging Representative Kahn in 2014. Ilhan even volunteered on his campaign, but by 2016 she had decided she herself would run for the seat.

In 2016, Mohamud and Ilhan were facing each other and the incumbent. The rivalry between the two Somali Americans made Ilhan's race more contentious than it would have been if Representative Kahn had been her only opponent, and it resulted in a drawn-out primary that eventually ended in her victory in August of 2016. But victory could have been hers four months earlier, at the endorsing convention of Minnesota's Democratic-Farmer-Labor Party (DFL). The DFL was formed in 1944 with the merger of the Minnesota Democratic Party and the left-wing Farmer-Labor Party (FL), which had been in existence since 1918. The FL had its heyday in the 1930s and 1940s, when it dominated Minnesota politics and its members were elected as governors, state legislators, and U.S. senators and representatives. The merger occurred under the guidance of Hubert Humphrey, who went on to become a nominee for president of the United States. The current DFL is the Minnesota arm of the U.S. Democratic Party.

In order to avoid a primary election, candidates for state legislature in Minnesota need to secure 60 percent of delegates' support at the annual state convention. In 2016, incumbent Representative Kahn, Ilhan, and Mohamud each hoped to win such an endorsement and avoid a primary race. At the end of a fourteen-hour deadlock during the convention, Mohamud had 11 percent of the votes, Representative had Kahn 33.4 percent, and Ilhan had 55.6 percent. She was only eleven delegates short of what she needed to eliminate the need for a primary, and if Mohamud had given her his votes, a primary could have been avoided. But Mohamud refused, and all three went to the August primary, where Ilhan won 41 percent of the vote.[5]

Both before and during the DFL convention, race, ethnicity, and gender bubbled to the surface. Representative Kahn, threatened by her upstart challenger, claimed that voters who supported Ilhan were doing so because of their "liberal, white guilt," which might be motivating them to support a person of color instead of supporting her.[6] Representative Kahn also suggested that Ilhan's success was related to her being "younger" and "prettier," a statement especially disappointing to the constituents who had long admired Representative Kahn for her feminism.[7] She had co-founded the Minnesota Women's Political Caucus, whose members helped identify, train, and elect pro-choice women throughout the state.[8]

Challenging an incumbent also meant going up against

conventional wisdom about how hard it is for newcomers to win against the political establishment. Reporters asked where Ilhan would find the votes, community leaders and other elected officials told her it wasn't her time, and party operatives didn't think there was a viable path to victory.

Within the Somali community, people told her she was naïve to think she could win, as a woman, especially since Mohamud had lost his three previous bids for political office. But win she did, and with 41 percent of the vote. She attributes it to running a campaign that was authentic and which put an end to the assumption that people would vote for her solely because they related to her identities. In fact, she says, people voted for her because they felt she represented their values. The campaign was built on economic, social, and environmental justice—on "realness and owning our narrative," as she describes it. Her big-tent approach to garner the vote from a wide range of voters was professionally run but also a family affair. Her father, then living in Somalia, was her chief fundraiser, and her son, then ten years old, introduced her at campaign events.

She outraised the incumbent by nearly 3 to 1, using surrogates within and outside her family to ask for resources to fuel her campaign.[9] Money came from out of state as well, from those who identified with her Muslim and Somali backgrounds. Seventy-one percent of Representative Kahn's contributions came from individuals, compared to 90 percent of Ilhan's.

To attribute Ilhan's victory simply to conviction, community enthusiasm, and progressive ideals would belie the sophisticated field program and targeted voter outreach that guided her campaign. Using a coalition strategy, the campaign mobilized multiple stakeholders to propel the win: young people, immigrants, and progressives. But beyond individual voters, the campaign spoke to organizers in the Black Lives Matter movement, the business community, local imams, and media in the East African community. They talked to individual and institutional gatekeepers in the community. The campaign mobilized around issues that directly affected these communities, including criminal justice reform, a $15 minimum wage, and engaging women in politics and business.[10] This crucial intersectional approach that took the connections between voters' multiple identities into account transcended singular identity politics, which might have led Ilhan to rely solely on a small base of women in politics or business, or Somali Americans.

The campaign's targeted outreach led to an increase in turnout of 37 percent compared to the 2014 election turnout. In the 2016 primary, overall turnout in Minnesota was down by over 120,000. But Ilhan's district was the exception, boasting an increased turnout of more than 1,500 voters.[11] Ilhan's campaign received nationwide attention from *Mother Jones* and the *New Yorker* because her election made her the first Somali American state legislator in the country.[12] But her campaign also demonstrated the potential that new American candidates have to mobilize a diverse electorate and win, even against established incumbents.

The path to victory over an incumbent is difficult, but it's not impossible. Ilhan's opponent had little experience with primaries after she was first elected. Prior to 2014, when she won the primary against Mohamud by 9 percentage points, Representative Kahn had never had a significant challenger in the primaries.[13] She likely underestimated her challenger's political sophistication and the district's latent dissatisfaction with her performance as their representative, factors that contributed to Ilhan's ultimate victory. Ilhan was the presumptive winner before the general election, since the district is safely Democratic and had been held by a Democrat for over forty years.

Initially, Ilhan struggled to gain endorsements from unions and support from political leaders. This is partly a function of groups wanting to stay on the right side of the incumbent, and partly a challenge that newcomers face to be seen as credible. After the primary, even some of the groups that had been reluctant to endorse Ilhan and to publicly voice support for her were eager to celebrate her, a signal of how easily an incumbent can win over politically powerful groups.

Since she won, Ilhan has also grappled with how her multiple identities play out in the public arena. She is a progressive community leader and organizer, but she is also the first and only Somali state legislator in the country. This may be largely incidental, but it is nevertheless historic. She is aware of this responsibility, and describes the difficulty of "represent[ing] something to the African diaspora at the same time that I must focus on the needs of people in my district." Whether or not she wanted to be, she is a role model for young Somali American women, some of whom have already told her they see her as a symbol of the potential they can achieve.

New political leaders like Ilhan Omar are particularly important as demographics change. Although 63 percent of the district that elected Ilhan is white, 18 percent is black, 12 percent is Asian, and the remaining 7 percent identify as Latinx, mixed race, or other.[14] Since Representative Kahn was first elected in 1972, her district's white population has steadily declined. But candidates like Ilhan aren't simply winning on the basis of identity; instead, they are using a formula that includes robust fundraising, targeted voter outreach, and relating to voters on core values. Charismatic and savvy, Ilhan also embodies multiple identities that are under attack in contemporary America—refugee, Muslim, female, black. She is exceptional, but not an exception.

On the same day that Ilhan won her primary, Fue Lee, a twenty-four-year-old born in a Thai refugee camp, also defeated fellow Democrat and twenty-year incumbent Joe Mullery for House District 59A in Minnesota. Fue won the primary by just over 300 votes in a race that drew 2,800 people to the polls.[15] The district has 40,000 residents and is 36 percent white, 34 percent black, 16 percent Asian American, and 6 percent Latinx. A notable 7 percent of the district is mixed-race. In Georgia's House District 101, political newcomer Sam Park won 52 percent of the vote against three-term incumbent Valerie Clark. The district he represents has 56,000 residents, who are 13 percent Asian American, 42 percent white, 22 percent African American, and 18 percent Latinx.[16] In San Jose, California, the tenth largest city in the country, Lan Diep defeated incumbent council member Manh Nguyen by 12 votes.[17] San Jose's population is just under one million, and three major groups make up almost equal proportions of the population, with Asian Americans and Latinx at 33 percent and whites at 28 percent.[18] In Anaheim, California—a city of about 350,000 residents that is 52 percent Latinx, 27 percent white, and 15 percent Asian American—Jose Moreno won a seat on the city council against incumbent Jordan Brandman by 72 votes.[19] In Arizona's House District 26, Athena Salman and Isela Blanc defeated incumbent Celeste Plumlee, in a district that has 215,000 residents, of whom 46 percent are white and 38 percent are Latinx.[20]

Overcoming the advantage that incumbents have, especially those who have been in office for the long haul, is not easy. Challengers often have to outwork their incumbent opponents by reaching new voters or those regular voters who have been ignored over the course of several election cycles. Tapping into the latent potential of first-time voters or those with a low likelihood of turning out is a key strategy for victory. In recent years, challengers have also capitalized on the frustration that voters feel with candidate choices that seem to represent politics as usual. Whether challengers ultimately win the election or not, their presence on the ballot serves to invigorate a race by prompting incumbents to sit up and pay attention, and by giving voters a reason to engage in a race that might have lacked any interest when there was no opponent, or when the opponent seemed to be just another example of the status quo. An incumbent who hasn't been challenged before may not only work harder during a campaign that becomes competitive, but might also be more likely to work harder once in office. Similarly, voters who might not have felt their

vote mattered when there was no challenger might be more
motivated to pay attention to the race and come out and vote.
Having a competitive race ultimately benefits voters, who get
a choice, and democracy more generally, by raising the stakes
and giving voters a reason to participate.

Just as challenging incumbents can yield successes for political newcomers and voters alike, term limits can ensure
that elections for open seats usher in new voices and boost
new and lapsed voter participation. Not far from Minnesota,
another young American Muslim also won his campaign, for
Michigan state representative, an elected position for the lower
chamber of the state legislature that helps set policy and bud-
gets for the state. Abdullah Hammoud vied with five other
people for the Democratic nomination after George Darany,
a three-term representative, faced his term limit. Abdullah's
other opponents in the Democratic primary included three
other Arab Americans and two white candidates. Abdullah's
story, like Ilhan's, is unique in its specific contours, but equally
American because of their shared immigrant heritage and determination to use their leadership voices in service of their
communities.

Abdullah's parents met in Dearborn; his father is Lebanese, but was born and raised in Saudi Arabia, and his mother
emigrated at age four from Lebanon before the start of that
country's civil war. When his mother, one of the first Arab
Americans in her school, started wearing a hijab at thirteen,
she was asked by her gym teacher to remove it during class.
To avoid doing so, her family asked an imam to intervene.
Decades later, Dearborn is home to thousands of natives of

Lebanon, Yemen, and Syria, but their numbers are hard to define because the U.S. Census Bureau still classifies Arab Americans as white.

Abdullah's mother dropped out of high school at age seventeen, after she married, but eventually went back to earn her GED. She became a successful small-business owner, operating a home and car insurance company. The Hammouds had four sons and one daughter. In October 2015, their eldest son died suddenly from a seizure, sending the family into deep mourning. One month later, Abdullah decided to run for the state legislature, partially in tribute to his brother. "My brother was my biggest advocate, and I wanted to be an advocate for the community in the same way," he said.

One of the many decisions Abdullah made when launching his bid for Michigan's 15th house district was what name to use for his campaign. The district has 88,000 residents, and 87 percent are white, with small percentages of Asian Americans, blacks, and Latinx rounding out the population. A large number of Arab Americans are counted as whites; but 39 percent self-report as Arab.[21] Another way to estimate how many there are is by looking at the numbers and national origins of the foreign-born. Approximately 15,000 people who live in the 15th District were born in Lebanon, Yemen, or Iraq.

Despite the large number of residents with whom he shares a heritage, Abdullah was asked by friends and local residents to consider running as "Abe," a shortened version of his first name. In the end, Abdullah made a bold and authentic choice to use his full name in his campaign. He says this decision was part of a personal quest to "make it okay for an individual with an identifiably Arab name to run and win in Dearborn," a reference that is partially directed at his predecessor George Darany, who is believed to be Arab American but doesn't publicly identify as such.

Abdullah's appearance is at once decidedly modern and somewhat old-fashioned. Sometimes he sports a scruffy beard, but his large tortoiseshell glasses and charming smile always dominate his face. Because of his light skin, he, like some other Arab Americans, appears white.

Arab Americans trace their origins to over twenty-two countries and number 3.7 million people. American Muslims are as diverse a group as Arab Americans are. Thirty-seven percent of American Muslims were born in the United States, and foreign-born Muslims come from seventy-seven different countries, sometimes resulting in nationalistic tensions within the community.[22] In fact, Abdullah suspects his Lebanese background may have lost him an endorsement from Yemeni elders in Dearborn, a by-product of the diversity within the Arab American community there and throughout the country.

Currently, Arab Americans self-identify or are categorized as white or other for the purposes of the U.S. census.[23] They can also indicate their ancestry as Arab, and those who are foreign-born can indicate their country of birth.[24] Piecing together this data helps to build a picture of the Arab American community, albeit an incomplete one. The U.S. Census Bureau was considering adding the new category of MENA (Middle Eastern/North African) in its question on race, to help collect more accurate data on these communities, but decided against doing so in January 2018, citing the need for additional research.[25]

Although spread out across the country, Arab Americans are most concentrated in the Detroit-Dearborn area, which, like much of America, saw its racial composition change dramatically over the last three decades. Former Dearborn mayor Orville Hubbard, who served the city for thirty-five years beginning in the 1940s, would certainly be surprised to witness the Dearborn of today if he were still living. He was well known for his campaign to "Keep Dearborn Clean," commonly believed to be about ensuring that Dearborn remained white.[26] Among comments attributed to him is "I'm not a racist. I just hate those black bastards."[27] Mayor Hubbard's negative views extended to other groups as well. In reference to Arab Americans, he's known to have said, "Some people, the Syrians, are even worse than n———s."[28]

The 1980 census indicated that 97 percent of Dearborn's 90,000 residents were white, and fewer than 1 percent were African American. Today, the population is only 7,000 people higher, at 97,000. Although 88 percent are white, according to the census's listed categories, 42 percent of residents claim Arab ancestry. The city's population is also 4 percent Latinx and 3 percent African American.[29]

It's particularly fitting, then, that the statue of former Dearborn mayor Orville Hubbard no longer stands in front of Dearborn's City Hall. Its removal divided the city as much as its presence did over the years, with some believing that Hubbard's contributions to the city deserved permanent recognition and others fiercely opposing ongoing reverence of his racist regime.

Abdullah feels Hubbard's legacy of racism in a deeply personal way, especially since he has come face-to-face with it often, most recently on the campaign trail. In February of 2016, Abdullah's campaign sent 7,400 mailers to residents who voted along Democratic lines or leaned Democratic in two of the past five primaries. Soon after the mailing went out, one of the fliers came back torn in half with "No Arabs" written on one half and "Go back to Lebanon" written on the other. Shocked but not daunted, Abdullah had his campaign issue a press release to share the story and put it on record. It was not the first time he had experienced racism in his own hometown.

Abdullah was merely ten at the time of the September 11, 2001, attacks and has formative memories of that day and the following days. "I remember 9/11 distinctly. That day, they let us out early. My mother, who wears a head scarf, drove to school to pick us up. In the car afterward, a guy cut us off, gave us the middle figure, and shouted obscenities at us." The next day, "as we walked to our middle school, another guy was looking out his window, drinking alcohol and pointing a gun at us, saying, 'Keep walking before I decide to shoot you.'" Harassment and discrimination continued through Abdullah's college years and beyond.

In 2014, after volunteering with the United Nations in refugee camps in Jordan, he was subjected to this line of questioning from immigration officials when he returned to the United States: "How long were you fighting in Syria? Who in your family is fighting in Syria?" These questions made racist assumptions of the type that make Abdullah and many Americans of color feel like second-class Americans.

Abdullah's decision to run for office despite being made to feel like an outsider is a marker of his dedication to his community, state, and country. His day job was to conduct competitive analysis for his employer, the Henry Ford Health System, which runs a hospital and an insurance company called Health Alliance Plan. Through this work, he learned about the shortcomings of the healthcare system and how the education system was failing young people. He was also active in state-level advocacy on the environment in his capacity as a board member of the Michigan League of Conservation Voters (MLCV), which endorses pro-conservation candidates for office. He knew that environmental groups like MLCV were not happy with the leaders or candidates representing the district, and all these factors and experiences influenced his desire to run.

Abdullah was not considered "the Muslim" in the race by voters and endorsing groups, since there were other American Muslim candidates running, and because of his relationships within the progressive Michigan world. Instead, he was seen as a progressive, like one of his opponents, Brian Stone. Brian was a formidable opponent—a gay Buddhist Navy veteran who was endorsed by Planned Parenthood of Michigan and the Gay and Lesbian Victory Fund.

But Abdullah bore the burden of difference, despite possessing similar politically progressive qualifications. When Brian proclaimed at a pre-election candidate forum that he (Brian) had five hijabis on his staff, Abdullah believed it was a perfect display of white privilege. Abdullah argues that, as an Arab, boasting about the number of Muslims on his campaign team would not be received in the same way. Abdullah responded to Brian by saying, "While it's great that my opponent is fighting Islamophobia from behind the podium and behind the camera, I'm living and fighting it every day."

One week before the primary election, Brian won the endorsement of the *Detroit Free Press*, a daily newspaper that holds unique significance because it is the paper read by many progressives. Its endorsements carry weight and can influence voters' opinions. A key section of that endorsement stated: "Hammoud and Stone are both promising newcomers who bring youthful energy and a sophisticated grasp of the issues to the table, but BRIAN STONE is better prepared to take on the responsibilities of legislative office. His advocacy on behalf of veterans and Arab Americans suggests that he will capably represent the 15th District."[30]

Despite failing to receive the *Detroit Free Press*'s support, Abdullah secured wide-ranging endorsements, including from the MLCV, the Michigan Chapter of the National Association of Social Workers, the Detroit Regional Chamber of Commerce, and the Arab American Political Action Committee, among others. These endorsements helped to inform voters, and in the end, Abdullah placed first in the Democratic primary, with Brian coming in 10 points behind, in second place. Abdullah went on to win the general election in November with 62 percent of the vote.

Abdullah describes his winning strategy as "doors and dollars," specifically referring to knocking on voters' doors and fundraising. Direct voter contact and money from multiple sources help to create multiple stakeholders in a campaign. He raised $130,000 from 603 sources, with the smallest contribution being $10 and the largest $1,050.[31] The campaign knocked on approximately 25,000 doors before the primary, and on 10,000 leading up to the general election. Ilhan's campaign similarly focused on door-knocking and small donors. She raised close to $110,000 in her 2016 campaign, and the donations ranged from small amounts to a high of $1,000.[32]

Like Ilhan, Abdullah is deeply connected and committed to his community of origin. And like her, he refuses to see himself solely as a voice for the American Muslim community. "We [referring to American Muslims] need one voice of solidarity," he has said, not one voice that only speaks for communities from certain countries of origin. In fact, Abdullah is forced to defend himself against critiques from Arab American and American Muslim activists that he is not vocal enough on a whole range of Muslim and Arab American issues, including the wrongful attribution of terrorists as Muslim. He struggles with this tension, especially because some in the American Muslim community have asked why he doesn't regularly post critiques on social media about incidents affecting them. Instead, he asserts that his decision to run for office and represent the district is as strong a statement as he could make about his commitment to the community. In the end, Abdullah and other legislators try to avoid focusing disproportionately on any subgroup of their constituents, both because they want to be fair and because they can come under more scrutiny than their white colleagues do for potentially being "the immigrant" or "the Muslim" advocate.

Still, as candidates and elected officials who come from groups that are underrepresented, they are motivated to speak on behalf of injustices against those communities. In a United States governed by Donald Trump, Ilhan and Abdullah are moved to be public voices against xenophobia and racism. In late January of 2017, while President Trump was signing one executive order after another to close America's borders and build literal and figurative walls, Ilhan was gathering Minnesotans together to hear her invitation to the president: "I want to offer an opportunity for our new president to come and spend a day with me—to see what it is to be Somali, to be Muslim and to be a refugee that has gotten the opportunity to have a new life."[33] A few weeks after his election, Abdullah took the oath of office with his hand on a Quran. The night before Donald Trump's inauguration, he took his fellow Democratic state representatives on a tour of the Islamic Center of America in Dearborn to introduce them to his district and residents.

Even as Ilhan and Abdullah live their personal lives as American Muslims, they must negotiate a public life in which they are serving those constituents with whom they share a religious background as well as everyone else in their districts. Just as white elected officials can serve diverse districts, so too can new Americans like Abdullah and Ilhan. At a time when American voters are clamoring for new, authentic voices, these leaders are connecting directly with their constituents' needs.

In his first year as a legislator, Abdullah introduced a package of bills and resolutions to expand immigrants' rights.[34] Ilhan was the chief author of twenty-five bills that addressed a range of issues including making Minnesota a sanctuary state, which would prevent local law enforcement authorities from enforcing harsh federal immigration laws there.[35]

Both legislators are exercising the leadership needed for these times. Rather than being asked to wait their turn by gatekeepers like newspaper editorial boards and incumbents, new American candidates need to be cultivated and supported by local political leaders, civic groups, and the institutions that provide resources to candidates. Unions and progressive organizations, which not only give resources but also provide volunteers to register voters and get out the vote, can help give candidates an advantage. To date, incumbents or well-established and well-connected residents are the ones who have had the most access to critical support. That needs to change, not just to introduce new voices but also to ensure a more robust democracy. A competitive primary—whether for an open seat or against an incumbent—can give voters a choice at the polls and keep incumbents from taking victory for granted.

Structurally, one way to open up opportunities for newcomers to local and state office is to institute term limits. Term limits have certain disadvantages, most notably that they reduce the number of people who have seniority and experience in state legislatures. On the other hand, term limits allow a regular infusion of new blood into legislatures and create openings for emerging leaders to bring their enthusiasm and energy into office. In the case of demographic changes in a district, term limits also provide an avenue for candidates who share racial backgrounds and life experiences with residents in their districts to represent them in legislatures. Nationwide, people of color make up 38 percent of the population but only 15 percent of all state legislators, a gap that could be narrowed if racially diverse newcomers had better chances of being supported for open seats or against incumbents.[36]

Without term limits, Minnesota's House District 60B was underserved by its long-term incumbent legislator, Phyllis Kahn, who took for granted that she would keep getting elected, and was eventually unseated by Ilhan Omar. With term limits in place in Michigan, someone like Abdullah Hammoud had the opportunity to run and win.

Another argument against term limits is that residents can always decide to vote someone out if they are dissatisfied with their representative, as was the case with Representative Kahn. Often, however, no one runs against the incumbent, handing him or her a default victory. Such a case allowed Representative Kahn to stay in office for forty-four years. Additionally, those in offices without term limits have little incentive to continue working for the approval of their constituents, since they know that voters have limited choices at the ballot box. This is what happened in Minnesota, prompting Ilhan to challenge Representative Kahn so that voters in the district would have someone fighting for them in the legislature.

Michigan is one of only fifteen states with term limits at the state level. In these states, elected officials in the state legislatures are limited to serving for a certain number of years, ranging from six to sixteen.[37] When they inevitably leave office, opportunities for new leaders organically emerge. Running against an incumbent is particularly difficult for first-time candidates, which is one reason why Ilhan's race is considered historic. Usually, the incumbent has name recognition from years of representing the district. Even the strongest new candidates stand little chance against established leaders who have been bringing adequate resources and attention to their districts.

In Michigan, term limits frequently bring in new blood. Senators can run up to two times for four-year terms. Representatives to the lower house can run up to three times for two-year terms. At the end of a legislator's term, multiple candidates will vie for the open seat, because they generally stand on equal footing with their opponents when it comes to name recognition.

Of course, even with term limits, new political candidates might still face the obstacle of gatekeepers. And naturally some candidates will be better known than others, able to raise more money than their opponents, or better networked than their peers. But most important is that no one has the "incumbent advantage." This levels the playing field.

Of the fifteen states that have term limits, only six have lifetime limits on serving in their state legislatures. This means that once someone has served her term, they can never run for the state legislature again. This prevents candidates from just taking one or two years off and coming back to run for the same seat they held before.

Since the pathway to Congress begins with local and state

office, term limits at those levels are an important catalyst for ensuring new political leaders emerge. But their ability to rise to higher levels of office is restricted without there being term limits for members of Congress, who often serve until they die or who retire after decades of service.

The lack of term limits explains why even the 115th Congress, the most diverse ever, is 81 percent male and white, while the country is 38 percent people of color and 51 percent female.[38] Three senators have been in office for more than thirty-five years, and in the House, eight members hold the same record. All but one is a white man. The only person of color, John Conyers (D-MI), is retiring in 2018 in the face of sexual harassment allegations.[39]

If legislatures fossilize into outdated versions of the population, their leadership won't reflect the interests or demographics of a changing country. Deep investment in the pipeline, starting from the local level and continuing through Congress, is critical to facilitating the emergence of more legislators like Abdullah and Ilhan. In state legislatures, they can hone their legislative skills, build name recognition and a track record, and develop stronger financial networks. Such experience sets the foundation on which to build a competitive run for higher office. Theirs are the voices that we need—at the state level today, and in tomorrow's Congress.

In fact, for Ilhan, that trajectory happened quickly. During her first term as state legislator in 2018, Minnesota congressman Keith Ellison resigned to run for attorney general. Ilhan is running for his seat, in the fifth congressional district, and may well become the country's first Somali American congressperson.

3

HIDDEN IN PLAIN SIGHT

Seventy-two became a magic number for Jose Moreno in November of 2016. That was the number of votes that gave him the lead over his opponent, incumbent Jordan Brandman, during a vote-counting process that didn't end until almost three weeks after Election Day. The razor-thin margin capped an amazing journey: Jose, an activist academic who was once undocumented, became the sole Democrat on the Anaheim City Council and only the fourth Latino in the city's 157-year history to serve on the council.

At forty-eight, Jose is tall and broad-shouldered and alternates between wearing T-shirts and guayaberas. He smiles frequently, despite a steely resolve. He appears easygoing, but can seem intense when talking about protecting his own—family, community, friends—from outside forces that would limit their access to opportunity.

Recently, much of Jose's resolve has been directed at the Walt Disney Company's outsize influence on Anaheim, the home of Disneyland. From streetcars to luxury hotels, if it's happening in Anaheim, chances are that Disney has its fingerprints on it. Disneyland may be known as the happiest place on earth, especially if you're a tourist or a wealthy resident, but many locals—service professionals, transportation workers, teachers—are forced into unpleasant fights with its corporate giant as they advocate for their economic interests. Part of Jose's job—first as a community activist, and later as an elected official—was to prevent his community from being swept up in the ever-expanding tentacles of Disney and its sister operations, which have a disproportionate impact on living wages and affordable housing for local residents.

Anaheim is a city of about 350,000 residents that is 52 percent Latinx, 27 percent white, and 15 percent Asian American.[1] Approximately one in three residents were born abroad, and nearly 69,000 of those foreign-born are Mexican.[2] Nestled in Orange County, whose residents have voted for every Republican presidential candidate since 1936, Anaheim is home not just to Disneyland but also to the smaller Knott's Berry Farm, another theme park designed to attract families with children.[3]

The city was founded by Germans in 1876, and was home to about 1,200 Ku Klux Klan members in the 1920s. KKK members briefly held four out of five seats on the city council in 1924 before opponents recalled them in a special election in 1925. As recently as February 2016, the KKK organized a rally in Anaheim that ended in violence and arrests. Anaheim resident William Hagen, also known as William Quigg, is a leader of the Loyal White Knights in California and other Western states.[4] Though the group has no website, it is listed as an "Active Ku Klux Klan Group" by the Southern Poverty Law Center, which tracks hate groups across the country.

Although Jose grew up in Oxnard, about two hours north of Anaheim, Disney has long been a part of his American story.

When he was four, his family baited him with the promise of visiting the theme park when they abruptly left Sinaloa, Mexico, for California. The ruse protected him from the truth: that his mother was in remission from breast cancer and needed to stay in the United States for ongoing medical attention. He didn't make it to Disneyland until he was thirteen. And three decades later, he became the poster child for fighting the Disney corporation, mostly by challenging the City of Anaheim. A December 2014 article about him in *The Orange County Register* was titled "How Much Does This Man Scare Anaheim's City Council Majority?"—a reference to a multi-year battle that Jose engaged in to ensure that his community had representation on the council.

Like millions of Mexican Americans and other immigrants, Jose's family turned a plot of dirt into a "street paved with gold." For more than a decade after moving to California, they were undocumented, like hundreds of thousand others, then and now. Given their legal status, these immigrants live, study, and often work here with the gnawing and constant fear that their lives could change abruptly if they are caught by local law enforcement or federal immigration authorities.

In 1986, when Jose was a senior in high school and getting ready to apply to college, the Moreno family benefited from a legalization program signed into law by President Ronald Reagan and commonly known as IRCA (the Immigration Reform and Control Act). The bill's seeds were first planted in 1977 by President Jimmy Carter, who asked Congress to consider legislation to assess penalties for employers who hired undocumented workers, increase border security, and create mechanisms for undocumented immigrants to gain legal status.[5] The path toward a final bill included resistance from members of Congress and later from a wide range of groups, including immigrant advocates concerned about possible discrimination against Latinx workers and labor groups worried about the impact on U.S. workers. After compromise and negotiation, a final bill passed in 1986 with provisions along the lines of President Carter's initial request: sanctions for employers who hired undocumented workers, and increased funding and requirements for border security.[6] The law also created provisions for over two million people to gain legal status.[7] This set Jose on the road to receive, first, a bachelor's degree from the University of California, Irvine, and then a doctorate in education from Harvard University.

Throughout his teens, Jose thought of himself as an American and was frustrated at his parents' inability to understand English well enough to navigate doctors' visits and the public school system. He admits to calling other Mexican immigrants the derogatory term "wetback," and feeling profound fear the day his mother was driven up to their house in handcuffs. The garment factory in which she worked had been raided, and as immigration agents brought her to their family home, Jose's father hid, fearful that he, too, would be taken away from the children, who would then have to fend for themselves.

Jose's mother was given a deportation order to leave the country within thirty days. "We drove to Santa Barbara, to a legal clinic run by Casa de La Raza, and a lawyer helped us find a loophole to [save] us from deportation," Jose says. Nevertheless, once the case was under full review, every six to eight months, the family had to appear before an immigration judge and answer a series of questions, including how each child was performing in school. This experience is unusual, possibly necessitated by the fact that a lawyer had found a loophole that allowed him to repeatedly appeal the family's case. But Jose thought this was a normal part of living in the United States.

Like the visits to the judge, other family practices seemed normal to young Jose. For example, his parents told him and his siblings not to open the door to anyone if they were home alone. The family closed their curtains when they got home, which the young Jose didn't understand was a way to stay private and under the radar of immigration authorities. They would practice the right intonation and syntax of saying, "I was born at St. John's," an area hospital, to deflect suspicion about their legal status. But these practices were *not* normal. They were part of the family's desperate attempts to protect themselves. In spite of participating in some of these practices, Jose really didn't know the details of the family's legal status, which he attributes to his older siblings' desire to protect him.

"We didn't learn English just to integrate," Jose says. "We learned it so we wouldn't get deported." That's the response he gives to people who tell him now that he speaks English so well. It's true, and it's a way of reminding people of all walks of life, including in politics, of the practical and psychological challenges that millions of immigrants face when they move to the United States.

Jose's organizing and activism stretch back to his years as an undergraduate. There, his student activism ranged from efforts to ensure equal access to university programs for low-income students and students of color to advocating for the creation of ethnic studies academic departments. As co-chair of M.E.Ch.A. (Movimiento Estudiantil Chicano de Aztlán, or Chicano Student Movement of Aztlán) and a peer ombudsman, he worked with fellow students to ensure equal educational opportunities for underrepresented students; help elect students of color to ASUCI (Associated Students of the University of California-Irvine), the student government body; to champion African American, Asian American, Latino, and Native studies programs; and advocate that "Greek housing" be broadened to theme-based housing that would allow students of color and the organizations that served them to be housed together and create enrichment opportunities for students not interested in, or welcomed to, traditional Greek life. The latter effort laid the groundwork for the creation of the Department of Chicano/Latino Studies and of the student dorm Casa Chavez, an academic theme house where students in the department could live and work together. Both the house and the academic studies program were established five years after Jose graduated.

He describes the strategy of student organizing as tripartite: including student groups, student government, and university leadership. The experience organizing students, engaging in electoral politics, and brokering conversations between formal and informal channels of power are all skills Jose continued to draw upon later in life, including in elected office.

After college, Jose went on to graduate school. Based on encouragement from a mentor and his family, he chose a partial scholarship at Harvard over a full ride at Stanford for his graduate studies. His student activism and experience within his own family and community had helped him see education as a pathway to progress. Not patient enough to be a classroom teacher, he decided to focus on education policy.

His decision to go to Harvard proved fortuitous for love as well. There, he met his wife, Lorena, who is from Long Beach, California, and is also a beneficiary of the 1986 immigration policy. After completing their doctoral work, they moved back to Long Beach. Once their eldest child was close to starting kindergarten, and their family had started to grow, high housing prices led them to move to Anaheim, which was more affordable and where they have lived since 2004. They have four daughters who have grown up attending Anaheim public schools, and Lorena is now a principal at a junior high school there.

Together, Jose and Lorena fought for resources for their own family and the extended Latinx community since they moved to Anaheim. Their first struggle started when they learned that, unlike in Long Beach, Anaheim's elementary schools didn't have a dual language program. They wanted their daughters to have the dual language experience, so they helped collect signatures from other parents to show support for the program. As they did so, they learned how monolingual Latinx parents struggled to interact with the school system, partially due to the language barrier.

Soon after, teachers at Anaheim High School approached Jose, whose doctoral research was on pre-college programs and their effectiveness for Latinx students, about the threat that a similar program—called Puente—might be eliminated at their school. By then, Jose had re-joined the community group Los Amigos of Orange County, which addresses issues of concern to Latinx and to which he belonged before leaving for Harvard. Jose and Lorena, along with teachers, community leaders, and newly organized parents, met with district administrators and spoke at school board meetings, resulting in Puente not only surviving the proposed cuts but also receiving expanded support.

As active community members and educators, Jose and Lorena were considered naturals to fill a vacancy that opened up on the Anaheim City School District in 2006.[8] The couple knew one of them should step up, but Lorena was hesitant. Jose argued that she was better qualified, with her experience in the K–12 education system. She argued that her job had less flexible hours and that she wanted to be around for their daughters, not tied up with the additional commitments that would come with being a school board member. Depending on your perspective, Jose drew the short or the long straw in the debate over whether he or his wife would run, and he went on to serve on the board from 2006 to 2014. In any case, although Jose's name was the one on the ballot, every election is a family affair.

Six years into his term on the school board, Jose began his journey to the Anaheim City Council. When the Southern California ACLU sued the City of Anaheim for violating the California Voting Rights Act (CVRA) in 2012, Jose served as plaintiff, along with Amin David and Consuelo Garcia, two other Latinos. At the time of the filing, Consuelo was an elementary school teacher, and Amin was a successful business owner. Both Amin and Jose were members of Los Amigos. The suit asserted that Anaheim's at-large election system restricted the ability of the Latinx electorate to substantively influence the outcomes of city elections. Not one Latinx was serving on the council at the time of the suit's filing, even though 53 percent of the city's residents were Latinx. Even more striking, only three Latinos had ever been council members in the city's 157-year history.

The CVRA, passed in 2001, provides even more protections to people of color than the federal Voting Rights Act does. The federal law, signed into law by President Lyndon B. Johnson in 1965, prohibits racial discrimination in voting.[9] The CVRA makes it easier for racial minorities to allege discrimination. Under the federal law, racial minority groups can't easily make a claim that an at-large system prevents them from electing someone of their choice. But under CVRA, they can. Furthermore, they can even claim that the at-large system affects their ability to influence the outcome of an election.[10] Most important, a plaintiff under the CVRA has fewer and less onerous requirements to meet to make a case that the election system is hurting racial minorities, whereas under the federal VRA, plaintiffs must demonstrate that:

(1) the minority group be sufficiently large and geographically compact to form a majority of the eligible voters in a single-member district,

(2) there is racially-polarized voting, and

(3) there is white bloc voting sufficient usually to
prevent minority voters from electing candidates of
their choice.[11]

Eliminating this requirement of the federal VRA makes
it easier for California residents to fight for district-based
representation.

Nevertheless, the lawsuit in Anaheim became a protracted
battle between the city and the plaintiffs. Anaheim is a "charter" city, which means any changes to elections must be approved by the voters. In a 2014 settlement, Anaheim agreed to
offer voters a ballot measure, Measure L, which proposed that
the city adopt single-member district elections. The settlement also called for expansion of council seats from four to six,
which went on the ballot as Measure M. Local groups worked
for months educating and mobilizing voters about the impact
of district elections on their communities. In November 2014,
both measures passed, with Measure L passing decisively, winning support from 68.3 percent of Anaheim voters.[12]

In 2014, before Measure L was implemented and while the
city's at-large system was still in place, Jose ran for council
and lost. That loss was partly a result of his having entered the
race very late. He had weighed the decision to run for many
months, concerned about whether it was the right decision for
him and his family. He was also reluctant to keep the spotlight
on himself, rather than on the larger issue of lack of representation for the Latinx community. But as the most prominent
voice on the issue, he was the one most often encouraged and
asked to run by community members. And he knew it would

allow him a platform from which to encourage voters to support Measures L and M.

Anaheim mayor Tom Tait is a moderate Republican who has been supportive of Anaheim's moving from at-large to district elections and has been willing to push back on some proposed policies that would benefit Disney, including imposing a twenty-year limit on an entertainment tax ban in 1996.[13] A businessman, Mayor Tait started as a council member on the Anaheim City Council in 1996 and was elected to his first term as mayor in 2010. In 2014, he served as the co-chair of the Immigration Task Force, a bipartisan committee of the U.S. Conference of Mayors, a nonprofit organization for mayors who govern cities with 30,000 or more residents. He is a vocal and ardent supporter of immigration reform, which would help give 11 million undocumented immigrants a pathway to citizenship, but which has remained elusive both because of gridlock in Congress and lack of support from recent presidents.

Mayor Tait and Jose have a strong alliance based on their similar views on these key issues. When the mayor was up for re-election in 2014, he invited Jose to run on his slate. As Jose stretched out his decision-making process, he lost some political capital. His final decision came in August 2014, well after the mayor had settled on a slate, leaving Jose with a very tight timeline for effective fundraising and organizing for his own run, and contributing to his loss.

By January 2016, when Jose was contemplating his second run, the Anaheim City Council was getting ready to approve the "People's Map." Drawn up to create, among other things, a "Latino district," the map was the culmination of years of negotiating that began with the lawsuit in 2012 and years of organizing by local groups, including OCCORD, a community–labor alliance founded in 2005 that focuses on bringing inclusive democracy to the county. Other allies included OCAPICA, the Orange County Asian Pacific Islander Community Alliance, which is working to enhance the health, social, and economic well-being of that community, and OCCCO, the Orange County Congregation Community Organization, a social justice community group.

Newly created District 3 is 72 percent Latinx, as are 55 percent of its eligible voters.[14] In November 2016, this majority-Latinx area of Anaheim would elect a council member. Would it be Jose, who shared an immigration story and ethnic background with so many of the district's residents?

His most formidable opponent was Jordan Brandman, who had been elected to the council in 2012, under the old at-large election system. Jordan had served as a trustee of the Anaheim Union High School District from 2008 to 2012, had a background in government and community relations, and had held jobs in city and county governments from 2011 to 2017. When Jose ran and lost in 2014 under the at-large election system, he came in fourth place among seven candidates for the two seats. In 2016, Jose was facing Brandman and four other opponents for one seat in the newly drawn District 3—where the Moreno family lived, where Jose's daughters attended school, and where Jose had secured the most votes in 2014. But it wasn't clear if home-turf advantage would protect Jose from Disney, which was supporting Brandman.

The Walt Disney Company depends on a range of services and supports, including transportation and hotel development, that require council members' support or resources to move forward. In order to preserve its interests, the corporation invests in the campaigns of candidates they expect support from once in office. In 2014 and 2016, the years in which Jose ran, the corporation broke its own record of campaign spending. In 2014, the company funneled $670,000 to PACs that in turn funded advertisements supporting "Disney-friendly" Anaheim city council candidates and opposing Jose and others. In 2016, $904,000 in campaign funding was traced to Disney. The funding eventually made its way to mailers supporting candidates like Jordan and opposing Jose, but the money first followed a circuitous pathway through groups like the Anaheim Chamber of Commerce PAC or Moving Orange County Forward.[15]

Once Jose made the decision to enter the race, he had Mayor Tait's support and ran an impressive people-powered campaign that focused on connecting with voters at their doorsteps and in small groups rather than on raising money and getting high-profile endorsements. His campaign team included youth and parents with whom he had worked, teachers, union organizers, and his daughters and their friends. He also garnered endorsements from what he describes as the two of the most "people-centered" unions in the city: UNITE HERE, which represents hotel workers, food service workers, industrial laundry workers, and other service industries, and UFCW, the United Food and Commercial Workers Union.

Although Anaheim is a big city, its districts are small towns now that the elections are district-based. Jose is a known entity in his district, as a teacher, a father, and a soccer coach. And, uniquely, he knows directly the experience of many of the district's residents, of whom 41 percent are immigrants. "Their friends are me and Lorena when we were eight, nine, fifteen, sixteen years old," Jose says. In the local schools, 85 percent of the kids are on the free and reduced lunch program, and many of them share the same concern that Jose's family did—that a parent might be deported.

Compare District 3 to District 6, which is only 19 percent Latinx and covers the affluent area of Anaheim Hills. The differences between residents of these two districts are stark: 29 percent of District 3 residents say they speak English at home, compared to 69 percent of District 6 residents. While 26 percent of District 3 residents make less than $25,000 a year, only 8 percent of District 6 residents earn such low incomes.

Jose had the profile of a strong candidate to represent newly drawn District 3. He not only shared the residents' demographic profile, he was also the champion of single-member district elections. Still, some unions withheld support, as did close friends who were also seeking political endorsements. Aligning with Jose could have meant alienating powerful union interests who had big stakes in Disney's expansion. The incumbent's endorsers included SEIU United Service Workers West and IBEW Local 47, the electrical workers union, in addition to the Anaheim Chamber of Commerce PAC and the Support our Anaheim Resort (S.O.A.R.) PAC. S.O.A.R. is a nonprofit that describes itself as a coalition of residents, business owners, and community leaders protecting the interests of the Anaheim resort district. In the last filing of their 2016 campaigns, Jordan had raised $184,000 and spent it all, while Jose had raised 75 percent less ($46,000) and spent $35,000.[16]

Alone, those financial disparities are noteworthy. But individual fundraising is only one aspect of campaign spending, especially in a city with such a powerful political player as Disney. Disney is only one on the long list of individuals and institutions that support incumbent Anaheim city council members. In this complex web of self-interests, some are more transparent than others. Anaheim is hardly the only jurisdiction where special interests are able to influence electoral outcomes by leveraging their checkbooks.

The landmark 2010 Supreme Court decision *Citizens United v. Federal Election Commission* dramatically changed the landscape for spending on elections. The court ruled that spending on elections is protected under the First Amendment as a form of speech and therefore cannot be regulated by the government. The decision meant that although corporations or unions could not contribute directly to individual campaigns, they *could* influence elections through other means, including the purchase of advertisements.[17] The money flowing into campaigns often doesn't follow a direct route. Each state has different reporting requirements for different campaign contributors. State super PACs are required to report their donors, but some types of nonprofits don't have to. "Dark money," the money contributed to political campaigns that can't be traced to its source, has become more prevalent in the years since the ruling, as has "gray money," the money that can be traced but requires sifting through layers of donors.[18] A 2016 report by the Brennan Center looked at election spending in six states that make up 20 percent of the country's population and are geographically and ethnically diverse: Alaska, Arizona, California, Colorado, Maine, and Massachusetts.[19] Two key findings are worth noting. One is that the lower costs of state and local elections allow dark money to have a proportionately larger impact than they do on higher-cost federal elections. The other is that the direct economic benefit of a corporation's relatively low spending in a council or state assembly race can mean tax abatements and decreased regulations in the corporation's district or industry. Most significantly, this "dark" or "gray" spending is layered, with one set of groups contributing to other groups, who eventually influence the outcome of elections by sending out mailers in support of their favored candidates or in opposition to disfavored ones. For example, a teachers union might contribute to a super PAC called Education for All, which could send out campaign mailers against a city council candidate who the union's leaders believe to be pro-charter. Names for PACs can be misleading or obscure, making it unclear where the group's political interests lie.

Jose's ability to surmount significant obstacles—lack of endorsements, incumbent advantage, and a major gap in fundraising—demonstrates the potential for outsider candidates to win elections with strong organizing and authentic engagement with the public and voters. His campaign had no paid staff, except for a fundraiser. The campaign manager and field director were volunteers, assisted by youth and parents who knew Jose and were enthusiastic about his election.

In terms of strategy, Jose's campaign focused on reaching out to voters who were considered "low propensity," or less likely to vote. For Latinx voters, Jose held "cafecitos," or coffee hours with voters in small groups, and he knocked on as many of their doors as possible. For Korean and Vietnamese voters, the campaign enlisted well-respected professionals such as doctors and school principals to do robocalls on behalf of Jose. Because funds were limited, the campaign was only able to mail one piece of campaign literature, which was sent to all the voters in the district.

In the last few weeks of the campaign, Brandman's supporters pulled out all the stops, saturating the district with paid canvassers and creating flyers with endorsements from well-liked Latinx elected officials. Hermandad Mexicana PAC, one of the entities reportedly funded by Disney, orchestrated this last push in an attempt to target Jose's base of Latinx voters.[20]

In the end, David beat Goliath, despite the disparity in resources, by that dramatically slim margin of 72 votes. Without a doubt, it was a gratifying victory—for a minute.

Soon after being sworn in, Jose learned that his seat had been randomly selected to be the one that would be up for re-election in 2018. Others would not need to run again until 2020, to allow for staggered terms for the incoming council members. (This practice allows each council body to have at least some experienced council members.)

Being a newcomer to the council didn't stop Jose from having a full legislative agenda. At the first council meeting of his term, he introduced two resolutions, one to make Anaheim a welcoming city, part of Welcoming America, a national non-profit initiative started in 2009 to ensure that America's cities are places where immigrants feel at home, and another to establish Anaheim's first-ever youth commission to assure inclusion of youth perspectives in the city's policy developments.

The council also took steps to block a streetcar project that would have cost Anaheim $270 million. The proposed streetcar was to travel over a three-mile track from the transportation hub to Disneyland and back. Jose and other opponents argued that the project was too expensive and would only serve tourists, instead of the broader Anaheim community. They opposed going forward with the project and agreed to explore alternatives that were more flexible and could serve workers traveling to Disneyland from around the city.

Finally, the council voted to end a policy that was initiated in July 2016 primarily to benefit hotel developers. Specifically, the policy allowed developers who built hotels with "Four Diamond" ratings to keep 70 percent of the room taxes they received for the first twenty years they were in operation.[21] Although the policy had already gone into effect, with some hotels grandfathered in, ending the resolution was an important symbolic vote and it sent a message that subsidies couldn't be taken for granted.

If one council meeting produced such productive results, what could be possible in two years' time? And what does that mean for Jose's re-election? Without any changes to election spending, the very Disneyland that helped lure Jose to America could cause him to lose his hard-won seat on the Anaheim

City Council and result in District 3's residents losing their most ardent advocate.

Jose plans to replicate AB 249, or the California Disclose Act, which mandates that campaign ads indicate their top three donors, even if those resources come through the kind of PAC mentioned earlier that bears an innocuous or opaque name. Though it is functionally a big step forward toward creating transparency in elections, the act only applies to state elections. Jose hopes to introduce an ordinance that would replicate AB 249 for local elections in Anaheim.

Some of his other activities include engaging neighbors and community members in conversations about homelessness, an issue that is connected to one of Jose's top-three policy concerns, affordable housing. The other two are raising low wages for workers in his district and curtailing excessive lobbying, which makes lawmakers susceptible to influence by well-resourced actors such as unions and corporations. Especially for legislators who only work part-time and have limited staff to research policy, lobbyists can become a source of information or data that is colored by their special interests. Glossy reports or well-funded briefings might influence policymakers to make decisions that are in the interest of the entity producing the report or the briefing, rather than in the interests of their constituents.

Institutional power in Anaheim lies not just with Disney but also with the major unions, like SEIU and UFCW, and with other elected officials in the city. Jose's core policy interests run the risk of alienating established bastions of Anaheim's power. His rise to a seat on the Anaheim City Council is especially ironic in light of the city's history of white supremacy. Despite his outspokenness and bold advocacy, Jose was appointed to serve as mayor pro-tem in January 2018.[22] In that role, he presides over the council's meetings in the mayor's absence, and represents the mayor at events.

Anaheim is a local manifestation of two heated national debates on demographic change and big money. One tension is between a history steeped in white supremacy and the current reality of a diverse electorate. The other is in the negotiation between corporate interests and the needs of working people. Jose is often a lonely voice on one side of these debates. His unwavering commitment to working-class people and the immigrant rights movement makes him both necessary and threatening. But imagine the potential for Joses around the country if the influence of dark or gray money were taken away. How many more community champions could penetrate a system that seems stacked against them today?

4

DOLLARS MAKE SENSE

On the blustery winter night before Donald Trump's inauguration in 2017, Isela Blanc, a Mexican American who lives in Arizona, addressed an audience of New Yorkers. It was her first trip to New York City, and she was unprepared for the cold, dressed in a lacy pink dress. Her face was deeply emotive, radiant and glowing, and her voice broke as she retold her immigrant journey.

Isela and the crowd of over 750 people were gathered at the "Anti-Inaugural Ball," organized by a group of progressive New Yorkers to benefit candidate-training organizations. Isela talked about living in a "crappy" two-bedroom house one block from the Arizona State Capitol as a child, and her disbelief that, over thirty years later, she had won a seat on Arizona's state legislature. Her story captivated the people in the room as they tried desperately to forget that Donald Trump would become America's new president the next day.

Isela had benefited from Arizona's Citizens Clean Elections Act of 1998, which provides state funding to candidates running for the state legislature and for statewide offices like governor or attorney general. Often referred to as public financing, this type of assistance helps to level the playing field for candidates who aren't independently wealthy and who would not otherwise be able to afford the cost of running for office. For Isela, an immigrant whose family struggled to make ends meet and build a life in America, public financing was her only entryway to running for office.

Well before she ran successfully, Isela benefited from a modest but idyllic childhood in Guadalajara, Mexico. Her mother tended a garden, sewed clothes, and stayed at home. When Isela was six, she moved to Oregon with her parents and two younger sisters. During her first year in America, Isela transferred schools three times, each new school in a different state. By the age of ten, she had been to schools in Oregon, Illinois, and Wisconsin. Her parents moved in pursuit of economic stability, more livable conditions, or better weather, and often in the middle of the school year. Every move was a gamble—with the elements, with the community, and with the schools.

Fortunately, the frequent moves and instability didn't hurt Isela's love of learning. "The best gift my dad got us was a set of encyclopedias," she says about her early years in Stoughton, Wisconsin. They were the only Latinx family living in a community settled by Norwegian immigrants in the 1850s and still predominantly occupied by their descendants. In 2018, the town is still 92 percent white, and it celebrates Syttende Mai, or Norwegian Independence Day, in May, a festival Isela remembers from her childhood.[1]

Both of her parents worked in an Ortega factory, one of several factories that created employment for residents of Stoughton and the surrounding towns. During the summers, she flipped through the encyclopedia's pages, losing herself in the written word. She walked one block to the local library and spent hours reveling in the worlds that books opened up for her. She looks back on the three years she lived in Stoughton fondly, especially when she recalls the well-resourced school system and the community that welcomed her. Then, in 1981, Wisconsin experienced a series of terrible snowstorms, repeatedly threatening her parents' commute to work. Isela's father, whom she describes as an adventurer, decided to try out Chandler, Arizona, where an aunt lived.

Arizona has now been home to Isela for nearly thirty years. This is the state in which she traveled the path from awkward middle-schooler to state legislator. At first glance, it might seem to be a classic "American Dream" story, but it's studded with bullying at school, economic struggle, and discrimination. Her entire family was undocumented until 1986. They had first come to the United States on a tourist visa to visit an uncle who lived in Los Angeles. For almost a decade, they lived on the margins.

When Isela was a freshman in high school, she had the same experience Anaheim council member Jose Moreno and millions of others had: then president Ronald Reagan signed the Immigration Reform and Control Act and created a path to citizenship for Isela and her family. She couldn't have predicted that a milestone in her American journey would later open the door to elected office. When IRCA was announced, Isela, as the eldest child and only fluent English-speaker in the family, completed the immigration application forms for all of her family members. A fourth sister had been born in the United States and was already a citizen, but the rest of the family took physical exams and gathered records to show that they had been in the country since 1982—the proof they needed to qualify for a pathway to citizenship under the law. Additionally, the family had to demonstrate a basic understanding of American history and the English language and prove they did not have criminal records. IRCA allowed approximately 2.7 million immigrants to become citizens, and it stands as the last comprehensive overhaul of the country's immigration system.[2]

Today, that law is a distant memory, in a hostile political climate that has made it difficult to engage in a meaningful conversation about a new immigration reform policy that would ensure a pathway to citizenship for the eleven million undocumented immigrants currently living in the United States. As a result of the 1986 law, people like Isela and Jose have become not only citizens but also deeply committed public servants. In Arizona alone, at least three formerly undocumented women were elected to public office in 2016. Isela was one. The other two, Ylenia Aguilar and Tanairi-Ochoa Martinez, both ran for school board seats. Each of them had a circuitous path to citizenship, but eventually both became citizens and, soon after, each filed paperwork to run for office. Poignantly, both women were eligible to vote for the first time in 2016 and won their seats on school boards in the first election in which they voted.

Arizona is believed to have only about 325,000 undocumented immigrants, fewer than seven other states have—including California, Illinois, and Texas.[3] But it is the crucible of anti-immigrant activity, as personified by Sheriff Joe Arpaio, who developed a national reputation as "America's Toughest Sheriff," and codified by SB 1070, formally known as the Support Our Law Enforcement and Safe Neighborhoods Act, but informally referred to as the "show me your papers" law. The law required anyone who was undocumented—or even looked like they might be—to present documentation proving their legal status to law enforcement officers. Passed in 2010, the policy put immigrants on edge, making them fear harassment and deportation. It also placed Arizona at the forefront of a national anti-immigrant conversation and served as a model for copycat legislation in other states. Sheriff Arpaio, a principal architect of the anti-immigrant environment in the state, gained national notoriety as an enforcer of the bill. Arizona state senate president Russell Pearce, the bill's sponsor, also gained national attention. When SB 1070 was being considered by the legislature, activism by Arizonans and Americans from around the country surged, with rallies and candlelight vigils. For many residents of the state, including Isela and her running mate in 2016, Athena Salman, the passage of SB 1070 marks a turning point in civic and political activism in their own lives.

In 2011, Arizona voters ensured that Russell Pearce, who had led the effort to pass SB 1070 in the legislature, lost a recall election (in which voters sign a petition for an early election in attempt to unseat someone before their term is over). In this case, Latinx activists in the state organized to help elect another, more moderate Republican, Jerry Lewis, an accountant by profession. Senator Pearce became the first Arizona state senator and the first sitting senate president in the country to lose a recall election.[4] He lost 53–45 to Lewis, who had been helped by nonprofit civic engagement groups in Arizona, including Promise Arizona in Action, Mi Familia Vota, and Citizens for a Better Arizona, who wanted to flex their political muscle in the wake of SB 1070's passage.[5] After a redistricting process in 2012, the district first represented by Senator Pearce and then by Senator Lewis has been changed.[6] Portions of it are now in the newly drawn District 26, a majority-minority district that Isela, Athena, and their running mate for the Senate seat, Juan Mendez, represent.[7]

Leading up to her decision to run for office, Isela underwent a significant political transformation. Like others who benefited from the 1986 Immigration Reform and Control Act, Isela registered as a Republican and voted along party lines for several election cycles. During that time, she also started college at Arizona State University and struggled to keep up with her course work while balancing a job at Chase Bank. At twenty-one, she dropped out of college, began working at the bank full-time, and married her high-school sweetheart, Todd. When they had their first child, she decided to work part-time so she could give her son the kind of care she remembered having as a child in Mexico. Two years later, they had a second child. With her part-time job and Todd's salary as a police officer, the family struggled economically, accumulating debt that they continue to pay off today.

In 2006, when her children were eight and ten, Isela left her job at the bank to care for her mother, who had been diagnosed with cancer. When she was ready to return to work, she made a career switch and began working in schools as a community liaison, for $10 an hour. Eventually, that led to a job with First Things First, a nonprofit that addresses a range of needs for Arizona children ages 0 to 5 to ensure they arrive to kindergarten healthy and prepared for success. As a subcontractor for the organization, she earned the highest salary she has ever earned, $64,000 per year, nearly three times higher than her current salary of $24,000 as a legislator. Given her income history and lack of social capital, Isela would not have been able to run for office without the help of public financing.

As she was navigating career changes, she also had a number of experiences that led her to the Democratic Party. Soon after the attacks of September 11, 2001, the anti-immigrant rhetoric of the Republican Party began to alienate Isela, who had thought of Republicans—in part because of the 1986 immigration policy—as being pro-immigrant. By the time of the 2004 presidential elections, she had become frustrated with other Republican positions that were anti-LGBT and anti-women.

Like other Arizonans of immigrant background, Isela was also deeply affected by the passage of SB 1070. The cloud of Arpaio sat over the state. An aggressive enforcer, the sheriff conducted raids to round up immigrants and promoted cooperation between local law enforcement and federal immigration authorities. He had violated a court order that mandated he stop profiling Latinos, and in August 2016, he was expecting a sentence of up to one year in prison for his criminal contempt of court. That same month, after serving as the sheriff for twenty-four years, he lost his re-election bid. A few months later, Trump pardoned him, and Arpaio is running for Senate in Arizona in 2018.

The aftermath of September 11 and SB 1070 informed Isela's political perspectives as much as they did Athena's, who is nearly twenty years Isela's junior. Olive-skinned and tall, Athena has a wide, heartwarming smile and dark, wavy hair. Unlike Isela, she was born in the United States. Their lives became intertwined in 2015, when they agreed to run on the same slate for Arizona's Legislative District 26, along with Juan Mendez, who had served in the state house since 2013 and is Athena's partner. All three participated in the Clean Elections program, and they campaigned together on one slate. They pooled their resources, making them able to do more for less. For example, instead of separate literature for each campaign, they produced flyers on which all three appeared. Leading up to the primary election in August 2016, their combined efforts reached 30,000 doors in the district, which has 77,629 households. Among the 215,000 residents, 46 percent are white and 38 percent are Latinx. Most of the district's residents—79 percent—are U.S.-born citizens.[8]

In Arizona, their strategy worked well in part because the Arizona House of Representatives has multi-member districts, with two representatives per district. When both seats are up for election, voters can make two choices at the ballot box. The two candidates with the most number of votes win the election, and Athena and Isela made sure they were the top two vote-getting candidates.

Athena's family is multiracial and includes her two

brothers, father, and mother. Her father emigrated from Pales-
tine, and her mother has Mexican, German, and Italian roots.
Her parents raised Athena and her siblings in Arizona, where
they now run a construction business. Athena was in the sev-
enth grade when the September 11 attacks occurred. "Four
days later, my friend's uncle was murdered at his gas station in
Mesa," she says, referring to Balbir Singh Sodhi, a Sikh gas station owner who was targeted in one of the many hate crimes
that followed the attacks. "I've been called Osama bin Laden's
sister, and my whole family has been treated as if they were on
the watch list," she says.

Shortly after the attacks of September 11 on the World
Trade Center and the Pentagon, President George W. Bush's
administration created and maintained a Terrorist Screening
Database, or "watch list." [9] A subset of that list is the No-Fly
List, which refers to people who are not allowed to board an
aircraft.[10] The Obama administration kept the list in place. It
is widely believed to be full of inaccuracies, and to randomly
profile members of the American Muslim, Arab American,
and South Asian communities. The exact number of people
on the list is hard to locate, with estimates as high as seven
hundred thousand.[11]

Apart from her mother, who kept her maiden name,
Athena's entire family, whose surname is Salman, had difficulty flying between 2001, after the attacks, and 2009. They
were unable to check in online, and, Athena says, at the airport check-in they "felt it was up to an individual to determine whether or not [we] were terrorist[s]." She doesn't know

definitively if they were on any list, an uncertainty many Americans have experienced.

Civil liberties groups have challenged the list since its inception in 2001. In 2010, the ACLU filed a lawsuit on behalf of ten American citizens and permanent residents whose presence on the list prevented them from traveling for family, work, or school purposes. After a protracted process, during which three other litigants were added to the lawsuit, the court ruled in June 2014 that the government's system for inclusion on the list was unconstitutional. In April of 2015, the federal government announced that it would tell U.S. citizens or permanent residents if they were on the list and "possibly explain why." The ACLU is challenging the constitutionality of the redress process, saying it denies meaningful notice, evidence, and hearing.[12]

After Omar Mateen shot forty-nine people at the Pulse nightclub in Orlando in June of 2016, the No-Fly List received renewed attention as Congress debated bills that would prevent people on the list from purchasing firearms. In this rare instance, the National Rifle Association, acknowledging that those wrongly on the list should be entitled to due process under the law, seemed aligned with civil liberties groups.[13]

For many, the policies of the Trump administration felt like a continuation of the nightmare that began in September of 2001. That may explain why, in the first week of the Trump administration, Athena and her fellow elected officials in Arizona stood firmly against restrictive policies that would close the doors to refugees and effectively profile Muslims. On January 27, 2017, the Trump administration issued an executive order that quickly became known as the "Muslim ban," barring the entry of citizens of seven predominantly Muslim countries: Iran, Iraq, Libya, Somalia, Sudan, Syria, and Yemen.[14] The executive order also indefinitely barred refugees from Syria and stopped entry of refugees from any country for 120 days. After being challenged in court and revised by the Trump administration multiple times, the Supreme Court will issue its final decision on the ban in the summer of 2018. In the meantime, lower courts have declared it unconstitutional.[15]

Responding to the xenophobic and unjustified executive order when it was first issued, Athena said, "It is immoral, it is unjust. America is diverse and we are stronger when we are united."[16] This statement is a reflection of her personal experience and an early sign of the conviction she would display as an advocate in the legislature.

District 26, which elected Athena, is where Athena first lived as a college student and where her political awakening as an adult took place. There, her diverse group of friends and colleagues give her connections that transcend ethnicity. The district she represents stands in contrast to her childhood home in a conservative, white, middle-class neighborhood near Scottsdale, where she was one of the few kids of color. Especially after the September 11 attacks, Athena felt isolated from her classmates.

Her experience is like that of many other American kids from immigrant families, who sometimes don't feel "different" until a certain encounter, or perhaps multiple encounters, makes it clear. Often these occur outside the home: name-calling by a schoolmate, an offhand remark by a colleague, or the discovery that, unlike classmates, they are ineligible for study abroad programs because they are undocumented.

September 11, 2001, was such a moment for Athena, certainly. But another momentous shift around her immigrant identity occurred in 2010, when the Arizona State Legislature passed SB 1070. For Athena, the activism before and after the law's passage helped her build solidarity with her immigrant friends while distancing her from some white friends. She describes becoming more aware that some people saw the police as a threat. And, she says, some of her white friends displayed their enthusiasm for the discriminatory law on Facebook. Her friends' social media posts served as a wake-up call for her about how they saw themselves as different from Latinos and other immigrants living in the community.

Given the state's demographics, SB 1070 effectively targets Latinos, who make up 30 percent of the population. Many have lived in the state for three, four, or five generations but were targeted nevertheless under the law. In 2012, the Supreme Court ruled in *Arizona v. United States* that three of the four provisions of the law are pre-empted by federal law and can't go into effect. But the ruling allowed the law's most chilling component to stay in place: the requirement that police officers in Arizona check the immigration status of anyone they arrest or detain.[17]

Before SB 1070, Athena had slowly been drawn into politics. Somewhat accidentally, or perhaps organically, her experiences as a student leader at Arizona State University (ASU) led her in that direction. As a first-year student in 2008, she focused on adjusting to college and was a member of Omega

Phi Alpha, a national service sorority that required twenty hours of community service per semester. She voted for Barack Obama in the general election but was angry that he picked then governor Janet Napolitano to head the Department of Homeland Security, because she was to be replaced by a conservative. Napolitano was a Democrat and had vetoed many bills that came to her from the Republican-dominated legislature, including bills that would have limited women's access to abortions and allowed people to carry loaded guns into bars and nightclubs.

With Napolitano in Washington, DC, Arizona's secretary of state, Jan Brewer, became governor, beginning a reign that included the passage of SB 1070. As all this unfolded, some political issues began to hit home. The state legislature massively cut higher education funding, leading the Arizona Board of Regents to pass a tuition hike for ASU students. Athena, a sophomore at the time, also had two siblings in college. She worried about how she and her siblings could stay enrolled, especially as both her parents had to leave college for financial reasons.

She says her parents emphasized the importance of education as a way out of the kind of backbreaking work they were still doing and wanted their children to be free of. Buoyed by her determination that she and her siblings should stay in college, Athena became involved with the Arizona Students' Association, which was organizing students to protest the budget cuts and tuition hikes. Later that year, Athena joined the Roosevelt Institute's Campus Network. The Roosevelt Institute is a national nonprofit that mobilizes diverse stakeholders, including college students, to reimagine economic and social realities that can work for all Americans. The Campus Network program organized summer internships at progressive organizations across the country for college students. As a summer intern at the Washington, DC–based Center for Community Change, a national, people-powered network for social change, she participated in work that contributed to the passage of the Affordable Care Act, and gained further insight into the world of organizing.

As a senior, she worked with the nonprofit Central Arizonans for a Sustainable Economy (CASE), which strives to ensure that young people and working families are able to achieve economic and social justice. The organization runs a number of campaigns, and Athena helped organize students to work on increasing Latinx voter turnout in Phoenix City Council District 5. This work indirectly contributed to the election of Daniel Valenzuela, a progressive Latinx firefighter who is running for mayor in 2018.

Though she had national and local organizing under her belt, Athena sought full-time employment in an economy suffering from the recession. She found it at a Westin hotel in 2011, where she worked as a service express attendant, alongside many others with bachelor's degrees who were struggling to find jobs in a post-recession climate. There, she joined the union UNITE HERE, the same union that lent critical support to Jose Moreno when he went up against Disney in Anaheim. Athena went on to become a union shop steward, an experience that helped deepen her knowledge about the injustices facing working-class people and introduced her to the tactics that people in power use to manipulate and suppress those who are dependent on them for wages or other resources.

By now, Athena had developed not only the experiences but also the networks that fueled a desire to be in public office. But the time for her to run didn't come until 2016, when she had even more organizing and community experience under her belt.

SB 1070 continued to be a part of Athena's journey, as was the case for many people of color in Arizona. The law profoundly affected the district that she now represents. Thirty-eight percent of District 26's population is Latinx. She had always felt deeply connected to both her Latino and her Arab American heritage. As someone with a multiethnic background, she saw the common threads of the immigrant experience. "My cousin has to sneak through the settlements in the West Bank to go to work, just like Mexicans cross the border to come to work here," she says. She believed the small Palestinian community in Arizona wanted the same things as everyone else: education and jobs. Still, she says, they do feel excited about *her* being their voice in the legislature, someone who they trust "won't stab them in the back."

Although being multiracial matters to her, Athena was most excited about representing her home state of Arizona. When she, Juan, and Isela knocked on doors, voters' responses varied slightly by ethnicity, but were mostly focused on the candidates' abilities to represent their issues. The high-propensity voters in the district—those more likely to vote—tended to be white and affluent, and were impressed that the

candidates approached them early. These voters also appreci-
ated the slate's focus on public education. Latinx voters had
similar interests, but also connected to the candidates based on
shared ethnicity.

Athena and Isela could focus on voter outreach early on
in their campaigns because they didn't have to worry about
raising a lot of money. Arizona's Citizens Clean Elections Act
requires that candidates like Athena and Isela—those running
for a seat in the legislature—raise $4,345 in "early contribu-
tions," which can include up to $740 of personal contributions,
including from family members.[18] In addition, they must raise
a minimum of two hundred $5 contributions from voters in
their district. Most important, none of this support can come
from traditional monied interests such as labor unions, PACs,
businesses, corporations, or political parties. This early investment in a candidate helps to qualify her for a state contribution of $16,995 for the primary election. The state provides
an additional $25,493 if the general election is considered to
be competitive. Connecticut and Maine offer similar clean-
elections programs, and New Mexico offers the program to
judicial candidates.

Another type of public financing allows candidates to fund
their campaigns with matching funds or small, direct contributions from voters or residents. For newcomers, both to
the United States and to politics, these programs help to level
the playing field, reducing the impact of established networks
that help position candidates or incumbents who are wealthy
or well-connected. Matching funds, in which states and localities provide equal funds up to a certain amount for each

candidate-solicited donation, is a critical public financing intervention. Hawaii and Florida have such programs for state elections. At the municipal level, New York City offers a robust public financing program, giving city council candidates a match of $6 for every $1 raised, to a maximum of 55 percent of their spending limit. Each donation can be no larger than $175. In New York City, candidates can also raise money from unions, PACs, and other institutions, but must also collect $10 contributions from seventy-five residents in their district in order to remain eligible for the program.

With the support of programs like these, promising new leaders from all across the country are getting the boost they need to run for office. Carlos Menchaca couldn't have won his seat for District 38 in Brooklyn, New York, without it. Carlos is a first-generation college student who moved to New York after college and worked as a government staffer. Although he had some connections throughout the city, it was his ability to match contributions that helped him raise enough money to run a competitive campaign. Like Athena and Isela, he defeated a Democratic incumbent in his first election.

In addition to matching funds, some jurisdictions have programs that allow local residents to contribute a fixed amount to candidates of their choice. Seattle, for example, implemented "democracy vouchers," which give $100 to residents who are citizens or permanent residents (green card holders) that they can contribute to political campaigns of their choice. The program is funded by a property tax approved by Seattle voters in 2015; it was first implemented in 2017. In that year's election, eligible residents were given four vouchers of $25 each, which they could use in the city attorney and city council races taking place that year. The vouchers could only support candidates who had agreed to accept donations of $250 or less. The program was overwhelmingly successful, tripling the number of people who donated to campaigns. Eighty-four percent of the campaign donors in that 2017 election were new donors, and 71 percent of those donors used vouchers.[19] This program helped to make democracy more inclusive by allowing any taxpayer—regardless of citizenship status—to contribute to a campaign. For new Americans, the opportunity to provide campaign contributions is a first step to engaging with electoral politics, even before they can vote.

While the details of each program vary by state and city, public financing programs often require that candidates demonstrate support from individuals within their district. That condition, along with other rules, creates a system of accountability and discipline for candidates. Most important, it frees candidates up to do the critical job of talking to voters in their district with the knowledge that their campaign is financed at the same level as those of other candidates (or at least at the same level as those of the other candidates who elect to have publicly financed campaigns). In the 2016 elections in Arizona, 23 percent of the 178 candidates for state office used the program in the primary election, and 26 percent of the 144 candidates who participated in the general election did as well.[20] From 2002 to 2010, participation rates ranged from 49 percent to 60 percent.[21] But reports from the Arizona Clean Elections Commission show declining rates of participation after 2012.[22] This marks the period in recent political history in which the role of super PACs has become increasingly prominent, following the 2010 *Citizens United* case. Since then, spending on campaigns by influential political organizations has increased exponentially. The U.S. Chamber of Commerce, which represents the interests of over three million businesses, spent $16.6 million on elections in 2008, and more than double that in 2012.[23] A similar comparison over two presidential election years shows that the League of Conservation Voters, which advocates for sound environmental policy, increased its spending from $2.5 million in 2008 to $11 million in 2012. Money is not given directly to candidates but is marked as "independent expenditures" on activities that advocate for or against candidates.

In addition, in the 2011 Supreme Court case *Arizona Free Enterprise Club's Freedom Club PAC v. Bennett*, the court ruled in a way that significantly changed the course of public financing in Arizona.[24] Prior to the ruling, clean-elections candidates would receive funding that matched what their opponents who were running in the traditional manner raised. But the Supreme Court saw this matching as a restriction of the First Amendment rights of candidates who are privately funded or are supported by independent political organizations. The 5-to-4 ruling allowed for the state's public financing program to continue, with limits. Faced with increased spending by opponents who are running "traditional" campaigns free from the restrictions of public finance programs, candidates in Arizona and elsewhere may be reluctant to "run clean." Although participants in the clean-elections program benefit from a lump-sum campaign fund and don't have to fundraise, they are also restricted from accepting contributions from PACs and corporations. If an opponent is running "traditional," candidates might decide it gives them a competitive advantage to do the same. Former president Barack Obama made a similar call in 2012, when his campaign signaled acceptance of super-PAC involvement in his re-election campaign.[25]

Despite super PACs, providing public funds to candidates opens up the possibility of running for office to those who lack strong financial networks or are not independently wealthy. Without the support of a program like the one in Arizona, Athena and Isela would have had to run very different campaigns or perhaps would not have run at all. Isela's decision to run, especially for the legislature, required overcoming her doubt about her capacity to lead, her qualifications for being in public office, and financial concerns. "In the political world, I'm an insignificant person," she says. Not being connected to lobbyists and special interest groups is one reason she feels she wouldn't have been able to raise enough money on her own. In order to ensure that her family can survive on her legislator's salary and she can remain independent of conflicts with any employers, her husband has taken on overtime shifts with the police department and off-duty work providing security at events.

For Athena, participating in the clean-elections public finance program made it possible for her to run what she describes as "a more authentic campaign," one focused on the issues affecting a majority-minority district. She says she would have felt more restricted from talking about issues she cared about, like racial justice and money in politics, if the campaign was focused on raising money from traditional donors. She is an ardent advocate for clean elections, and believes strongly that women of color especially benefit from public financing because "We don't have the money to run." When she speaks about the opportunities offered to candidates of color because of the clean-elections program, she is zealous, especially now that she has benefited from the program.

As candidates, Isela and Athena designed a strategy that allowed them to overlap fundraising with direct voter contact. They raised their initial $5 contributions by talking to voters in the district, who were the only ones eligible to give toward that requirement. The program also allows candidates to raise an initial $4,000 in seed money from anyone who is a U.S. citizen. Both of them drew on the financial support of their family and friends, within and outside Arizona, to meet that goal. "We used that money to print our first literature pieces," Athena says. Once the early requirements had been met, they were able to focus on voter contact. Athena stressed that the freedom to focus on voters early on, without the pressure of fundraising, meant that they could direct their energy toward voters who didn't turn out regularly. These low-efficacy voters are often low-income and people of color and tend to live in precincts ignored by traditional candidates, who focus on the prime voters, or those who are more affluent, informed, and connected to the political process. This is a vicious cycle, in which those who are approached keep turning out to vote, and candidates keep reaching out to people who show up to vote. Those who don't show up at the polls often get ignored by candidates, and thus continue to be on the margins of democracy. Candidates like Athena and Isela, who are similar in profile to, or familiar with, low-efficacy voters, are more likely to reach out to them, expanding the electorate in the process.

In fact, this is precisely what happened in their 2016 elections. The combined efforts of the three candidates on the slate led to a 23 percent increase in voter turnout in the August primary (from 2014) and officially took the district from being Democratic-leaning to Democratic. Athena and Isela won two seats in the Arizona House primary despite not being endorsed by the AFL-CIO, Planned Parenthood, Sierra Club, or the Arizona Education Association.[26] All four of these organizations endorsed the incumbent, who had been appointed to the seat six months before the election. Even as women of color who had been active in their communities prior to the election, Athena and Isela still could not overcome the favoritism given to incumbents by progressive endorsing institutions. These endorsements matter not just for credibility but also for the "people power" and the resources they bring to campaigns. Since they were running as part of the clean-elections program, the two women wouldn't have been able to take funding from the organizations that endorsed the incumbents, but the stamp of approval might have helped make them better recognized in the community. Instead, the incumbent, Celeste Plumlee, who had chosen not to participate in the clean-elections program and who raised $30,000 for her campaign, also benefited from being endorsed. Celeste's campaign literature referred to Athena and Isela as "dirty politicians," a comment tinged with racial overtones, marking one of the ugly ways race played into the campaign.

House District 26 includes parts of the city of Phoenix, which is 46 percent white, like the district is. But it also includes the cities of Tempe, which is 60 percent white, and Mesa, which is 65 percent white.[27] It's in these areas, where the percentage of whites is greater than in the district overall, that the idea of three candidates of color felt more threatening. Isela believes that some of the tensions that arose during their campaigns reflect the discomfort that white Democrats feel with new Americans "encroaching on white power." One white voter said to Athena, "This feels like a hostile takeover," referring to Athena, Isela, and Juan, all of whom are people of color.

But thousands more helped to elect them, making them, according to Isela, "the brownest people [in power] this far east" in Maricopa County. In fact, when Isela's parents had saved enough money to buy a home in 1980, their real estate agent actively discouraged them from buying in Tempe, pushing them to live in Phoenix, which was more racially and economically diverse.

Athena and Isela embody both the opportunities and challenges inherent in our changing demographics. On the one hand, their presence on the state legislature demonstrates that it's possible to break into the political system, even as newcomers. On the other hand, Isela wouldn't have run without the help of public financing. Their example points to the strong potential for change in the type of legislator we can elect to serve the needs of Americans who are ethnically diverse and economically fragile.

Voices like theirs can help unify people around a more inclusive vision for America, one in which everyone, regardless of immigration status, race or ethnicity, class or gender, feels not only motivated, but able, to participate. When Isela visits classrooms, students who are currently undocumented express hope about the possibility and potential of America's democracy. People like Athena, who are multiracial or victims of post-9/11 harassment in schools, workplaces, and airports, can see someone like themselves helping to shape policy for this generation and the next. These voices bring an intersectional perspective to state capitols that is sorely lacking—that of first-generation college students and women of color familiar with the difficulties of building a life with economic stability and social mobility. But without public financing, they would be outside of state capitols rather than in them influencing policy. Their elections moved them forward, but more importantly, also amplified the voices of thousands in their district and in Arizona who have had similar experiences and now have champions in the legislature.

5

THE COSTS OF PUBLIC LIFE

When Carmen Castillo moved to the United States from the Dominican Republic in 1993, she could not have imagined the life she would one day lead. Carmen settled in Providence, Rhode Island, with her three daughters and began working at a factory. Soon after, she began work as a room attendant at the Westin hotel, where she joined a union, eventually rising to leadership positions as steward and member of the executive board.

As a mother and community resident, she fought school closings and worked to improve the conditions of Providence's public schools. This activism and her union leadership set the stage for a historic run for Providence City Council. In January 2012, Carmen became the first hotel worker to serve on the council of a major city, and in 2014, she was re-elected to a second term representing Ward 9. That district includes the neighborhood of Elmwood, on the other side of the river from Brown University. Although 45 percent of Providence is Latinx, a demographic reflected in Ward 9, much about Elmwood is different from the city in which it sits. The city's median annual household income is $40,000, whereas Elmwood's is $34,000; average household size in Providence is 2.8 people, but in Elmwood, it's 9.0; and although 29 percent of

Providence is foreign-born, 45 percent of Elmwood's residents were born outside the United States.[1]

By day, Carmen vacuums hotel rooms and wears rubber gloves to arrange guests' personal belongings neatly. On the first and third Thursday of each month, she presides over council meetings. Carmen is not the image that comes to mind when most people think of an elected official. Often, the American public imagines the life of a legislator as some version of "leisurely" or "wealthy." That may be true for a select few, in federal office especially, but many elected officials must settle for some financial instability or uncertainty when they decide to run for office. Others, like Carmen, balance jobs with their public service.

Across the country, Yvanna Cancela, who was the political director at the Culinary Workers Union (CWU) before becoming a state senator in Nevada, makes $8,777 a year plus a per diem allowance for the days on which the legislature meets. In Nevada, that's 120 days every two years. Yvanna explains that it's "more prohibitive than representative" to have a legislature that pays so little, meets so infrequently, and relies on a flexible work schedule.

A life in public office in America is draining, in part because of a 24/7 news cycle that can require immediate responses from public figures. Whether a bill is being considered on the floor of a legislature or a tragic accident occurs, elected officials are expected to be available to respond, in addition to regularly engaging their constituents through social media. They are also under constant pressure to see and be seen—at community events, for fundraising purposes, and at their district's businesses.

As they juggle these public lives, legislators are often paying a personal price for their decisions, sometimes living at the margins of the economy as they struggle to survive on part-time salaries for full-time jobs. On the one hand, they must fulfill their responsibilities to their constituents, as it is the main reason most people choose to run and the primary way to ensure they remain in office. On the other hand, the constant demands of their public roles can restrict their ability to maintain other meaningful employment to augment the low wages most legislators receive. Americans from minority and immigrant communities are often the most likely to struggle with questions about their financial stability before deciding to take on a role in public life and serve in office.

Jessie Ulibarri, who served in the Colorado State Senate from 2012 to 2016, is baby-faced and dark-haired. Openly gay, Jessie is a passionate social-justice advocate whose political activity began in college. Often dressed in plaid shirts and jeans, he presents humbly, frequently referencing his early childhood in a trailer park. While serving as a senator, he annually took one week to live on a limited budget to remind himself what it was like for his constituents on food stamps. But even for him, living on a state senator's annual salary of $30,000 was a struggle. The Colorado General Assembly expected 120 days of his time and paid an additional $45 per diem for days it was in session.

Jessie's maternal grandparents are from Finland and Croatia,

and his father is *puro Chicano*, a descendant of the soldier and
explorer Juan de Ulibarrí, who was born in San Luis Potosi,
Mexico, in 1670 and found his way through New Mexico to
Colorado in 1706.

Nearly three hundred years later, in the fall of 2001, Jessie
began attending the University of Colorado Boulder. During the previous summer, his father, a construction worker,
was injured on the job, tearing all the ligaments in his knee
and shattering his shoulder blade. Unable to work, he couldn't
help with Jessie's college expenses. The family had never been
wealthy, but they earned enough that Jessie didn't qualify for
financial aid. After his father's accident, Jessie's freshman year
became much more financially challenging. He took on three
part-time jobs on campus, balancing his academic responsibilities as a student with being a resident advisor, a community outreach liaison at the GLBT Resource Center, and an
administrative assistant for the President's Leadership Class, a
four-year leadership program for outstanding undergraduates.
All of his jobs gave him deeper insight into his fellow students'
needs. Perhaps because of this, and despite his overfilled work-
load, Jessie was poised to become more active on campus. In
the middle of his first year, Colorado's legislature proposed to
dramatically increase the tuition that students at all state colleges and universities were paying. Jessie was spurred to action.
Through lobbying with other students, he was able to help
defeat the bill. Then, Jessie ran his first successful campaign—
for Leslie Herod, an African American woman who went on
to serve as president of the Legislative Council. Leslie later

pursued a career in political office and was elected to the Colorado House of Representatives in 2016.

During his time in student government, Jessie served as the legislative affairs liaison. Here, his activism became more public when he testified at the state legislature in 2003 to advocate that undocumented students receive the benefit of in-state tuition. Anti-immigrant legislators were a vocal and organized force in Colorado at the time; when undocumented residents testified at the bill's hearing, Republican legislators reported them to immigration authorities. The issue of in-state tuition languished in the legislature for ten years. Jessie was a state senator when Colorado finally approved in-state tuition for undocumented students in 2013.

During that ten-year period, Jessie racked up an illustrious career of activism, much of it during his student years. While he was advocating in the legislature, he was leading electoral efforts for the United States Student Association (USSA), the country's most established student organizing group. The organization describes itself as preparing "lifelong leaders at the forefront of making social change," an apt description of Jessie. During his involvement with USSA, he ran for and won the role of chair of the group's National Queer Student Coalition and served on the national board of the organization. As a representative of USSA, he went to Washington, DC, to lobby for the first version of the DREAM Act, which would create a path to citizenship for undocumented students. At the same time, he was pushing for pro-immigrant legislation in his home state.

After graduation in 2006, he received a nine-month public policy fellowship from the Congressional Hispanic Caucus Institute (CHCI), which offers Latinx college graduates an opportunity to work in Washington, DC. Jessie was placed in the office of an immigrant rights advocate from Illinois, Rep. Luis Gutierrez. He describes that experience as inspiring but ultimately disappointing, in no small part because Congress was active on a number of bills on immigration but could not pass any legislation.

From 2005 to 2007, legislative activity in Congress, advocacy by immigrant rights groups, and rallies and protests by immigrants and their allies fueled the movement for comprehensive immigration reform, or CIR. Ideally, CIR would be a "three-legged stool," which meant it would secure borders, provide a pathway to citizenship for the estimated 11 million undocumented immigrants in the country, and establish a plan for future migration.[2] Several bills were introduced in the Senate and House, including the Secure America and Orderly Immigration Act of 2005, often referred to as the McCain-Kennedy bill after its sponsors, and the Comprehensive Immigration Reform Act of 2006. The period marks a time of optimism and heightened activity among advocates for immigration reform, who then saw their hopes, and those of millions of immigrants, crushed as both houses of Congress were unable to agree on any bill.[3]

On the heels of that disappointment, Jessie returned to Colorado and started working for the Colorado Progressive Coalition, an affiliate of National People's Action, a network of grassroots organizations that engage in direct action for economic and racial justice. He held several other roles at nonprofits, including at the immigrant rights group Mi Familia Vota, which helped to mobilize Latinx voters in the 2010 elections, and at the Colorado branch of the ACLU, where he helped to create its first public policy program. Always the overachiever, Jessie was also active outside of his paid work. He and Julie Gonzales, who is running in 2018 for Colorado State Senate, started the Colorado Latino Forum in 2009, with the goal of increasing political power for Latinx. The group's efforts in 2011 ensured that Latinx voices were heard during the redistricting process as new districts were being considered and created. Through those efforts, a new senate seat was drawn for the state, a seat for which Jessie would run in 2012.

In the years leading up to the election, the political backdrop in Colorado was informed by the passage in 2006 of SB 90, a "show me your papers" law that predominantly targeted the Latinx community, which made up 20 percent of the state's population. The law effectively encouraged local law enforcement officers to report to federal immigration authorities any immigrant they arrested who was in the United States without the appropriate documents.[4] Colorado's law was on the books until 2013, when governor John Hickenlooper approved its repeal, but it flew largely under the national radar, unlike Arizona's SB 1070. Passed in 2010, Arizona's bill is widely considered to be the model for at least twelve copycat bills across the country.[5] Colorado's SB 90 was among the many anti-immigrant bills passed in the country between 2005 and 2012, emerging in part due to lack of action on immigration reform at the federal level. National anti-immigrant groups like

NumbersUSA and the Federation for American Immigration Reform (FAIR), both of which promote restricting immigration to the United States, found sympathetic ears among legislators like Arizona's former state senator Russell Pearce.

In Colorado, Jessie's frustration with policy was coupled with his disappointment with elected officials. He had worked for and admired Mark Udall when he was in the Colorado House of Representatives. The Udalls are a prominent political family in several western states including Colorado, New Mexico, and Utah. Mark worked at the nonprofit Outward Bound, which provides outdoor education for youth and adults, for twenty years before he ran for office. After one term in the state legislature, he went on to serve in Congress, first in the House and then in the Senate. But early in his tenure in Congress, Udall voted in favor of H.R. 4437, an enforcement-only bill commonly referred to as the Sensenbrenner bill, for Wisconsin Rep. Jim Sensenbrenner. The bill passed the House in 2005 but died in the Senate. Still, Udall's support for the bill, which would have increased border security and made it a criminal offense to be in the United States without documentation, crushed Jessie.[6]

In December 2008, President Barack Obama chose Colorado senator Ken Salazar to lead the Department of the Interior, which is tasked with maintaining federal lands and national resources, as well as administering programs related to Native Americans and Alaskan and Hawaiian Natives. Salazar's vacancy in the Senate was filled by then governor Bill Ritter; he appointed Michael Bennett, a lawyer and businessman who had been serving as the superintendent of Denver

Public Schools. Jessie was discouraged by the replacement of a Latinx representative by a straight white male instead of one of the many qualified people of color and women who could have filled the seat. The vacancy at Denver Public Schools, whose students are 56 percent Latinx, was filled by Tom Boasberg, another white male.[7] Jessie's frustration about these appointments, his passion for policymaking, and his prominence in Colorado all primed him for his senate run.

The right moment came in 2011. Following the 2010 census, Colorado's reapportionment process resulted in the creation of a new senate seat where Jessie lived. His mother had been raised on the west side of the district, which is predominantly white, and his father on the east side, which is predominantly Latinx. As a child, Jessie lived in the middle of the district. Because of this, plus his impressive track record on immigrant rights advocacy as a student, his work on electoral politics among Latinx, and his community leadership, he was perfectly positioned to run for office.

When he decided to run, he was earning $75,000 a year as a policy director at the ACLU, a salary he describes as "more than my parents earned together at any time in their life." In order to avoid any accusations of conflict of interest, he stepped down from the job. Once he declared, two potential competitors, both white and older, chose to stay out of the race.

Thanks to his work with Senator Udall and Mi Familia Vota and his deep roots in Colorado, he raised $30,000 in four weeks and racked up endorsements from elected officials and unions. Through his campaign and first year in the legislature, he worked for a nonprofit consultancy and made $40,000 a year. But as his legislative career matured and his family grew, the pressures mounted.

A politically active state senator might seem highly employable, but Jessie's primary potential employers in Colorado—nonprofits—were wary. He understood their skittishness. Nonprofit organizations are expected to be nonpartisan, and while employing an elected official is not explicitly political, it can be interpreted as favoring one party over the other, or as currying the favor of a sitting elected official. An organization could be seen as attempting to influence the outcome of legislation by employing a legislator who would later be voting on a bill that affected the organization or its members. Hiring legislators belonging only to one political party, even if their job was to conduct the business of the organization, could be seen as "a political act" and bring unwanted or unwarranted scrutiny from the Internal Revenue Service.

Jessie's partner, Louis, to whom he is now married, was trained as an airport mechanic. He worked with Southwest Airlines and maintained flexibility to offset childcare expenses and be around while Jessie worked days, evenings, and weekends. Luis's teenage son lived with them, and in May 2011, their second child, Silvia, arrived. They purchased a home during the foreclosure crisis in Adams County, a stable and solidly Democratic county that is 38 percent Latinx.[8] The hardest times financially were when Jessie was out of session, when the per diem provided by the legislature couldn't supplement their daily expenses.

Being a state or local legislator not only doesn't pay enough, it also costs money. Going to events and community meetings; attending dinners; buying and cleaning suits; and purchasing a car and using gas to travel to and from events are all expenses legislators are expected to shoulder on their own. Even when the legislature is in recess, they have to have a presence in the community, fundraise, and build up a campaign account.

For Jessie, those pressures were compounded by the everyday financial priorities that come from parenting and owning a home. For a time, the financial pressures eased when he got a flexible job with Wellstone Action, an organization created to honor the legacy of former Minnesota senator Paul Wellstone, who died suddenly in a plane crash in 2002. Wellstone prepares individuals and organizations to run and lead with the same progressive values that Senator Wellstone was known for, and Jessie traveled the country leading campaign trainings for the organization.

He had asked not to work in Colorado to avoid any potential of conflict, so he spent his weekends working out of state as a trainer. During the week, he juggled parenting and his legislative responsibilities. Over five years, he had roughly twenty days off, including the time he took off for holidays, his wedding, the adoption of a child, sick time, and the general time it took to be an active member of his family. Unable to sustain this pace, Jessie decided not to run for re-election in 2016.

In neighboring Arizona, where Rep. Athena Salman was elected to the state legislature in 2016 while using the state's Clean Elections program, the situation wasn't much better. Both Athena and her partner, Juan Mendez, the state senator, earn $24,000 a year plus a per diem of $35 a day for the first

120 days that the legislature is in session and $10 a day for additional days or special sessions. A typical legislative session runs for one hundred days, or until a budget is passed. Those days can be long, filled with community meetings, hearings, and negotiations. As Democrats, Juan and Athena are faced with a Republican majority that is obstructionist, making their jobs not just low-paying but also challenging. Juan has been in office since 2012, and has balanced being a legislator with several part-time jobs, including teaching at Phoenix Community College, doing deliveries for Amazon, and running a small nonprofit. These supplemental jobs help him make a living and pay off student and campaign debt. After her first session with the legislature, Athena returned to work for the nonprofit Central Arizonans for a Sustainable Economy (CASE), where she had worked as a senior in college. While she is actively campaigning for re-election, she will not be able to keep the nonprofit job, to avoid any appearance of partisan activity on CASE's part.

Carmen Castillo, Juan, Athena, and Jessie are not outliers. Yakima council member Carmen Méndez makes $1,075 a month and also holds a full-time job in the nonprofit sector to have an adequate living standard. Jose Moreno earns $46,459 per year on the Anaheim City Council, but also needs to maintain full-time employment as a professor at Cal State Long Beach to support his family and cover the high cost of living in California. Minnesota state representative Ilhan Omar earns a salary of $31,492 a year and also works in the nonprofit sector to supplement her income.

These low salaries are no coincidence and indeed a legacy

established by the founding fathers at a time when the expectations of legislators were very different than they are today, and as a bulwark against the kind of public servant focused on their self-interest. Thomas Jefferson, in 1797, said the following:

> All can be done peaceably, by the people confining their choice of Representatives and Senators to persons attached to republican government and the principles of 1776, not office hunters, but farmers whose interests are entirely agricultural. Such men are the true representatives of the great American interest, and are alone to be relied on for expressing the proper American sentiments.[9]

But legislatures populated by farmers are no longer the norm, and certainly not a reflection of today's "great American interest."

To be fair, some state and local politicians who earn full-time salaries receive wages that are higher than the median American income of $59,039.[10] In the four states with full-time legislatures, the yearly salaries are $90,526 in California, $84,012 in Pennsylvania, $79,500 in New York, and $71,685 in Michigan. These salaries are supplemented with per diem allowances for days the legislatures are in session. The total incomes hardly inspire sympathy.

But these numbers alone don't tell the full story. Legislators' take-home pay is one element of a journey that is more complicated for these first-generation elected officials. Like Detroit city council woman Raquel Castañeda-López, they may still live at home and help support siblings. They are also often the first member of the family to have completed college, hold a white-collar job, and travel in circles never before open to them as low-income Americans.

For Carmen Méndez, this new world included having dinner in what she describes as a mansion with the owners of a packing plant, the same plant her mother had worked in for decades. Her status as a Yakima city council member was the only thing that allowed her such access. In some ways, this represents the kind of opportunity that is only possible in America. But another side of this American story is that Carmen's mother must continue her backbreaking work even as she ages.

In some cases, people postpone running for office until later in life, when they have achieved greater financial stability. Vandana Slatter, for instance, a Washington state representative, waited until she could afford to quit her job and her son was out of high school before she ran for the Bellevue City Council. Until December of 2016, councilmembers made $19,800 a year, a salary that had not increased for sixteen years. When the salaries increased in 2017, media reported a "45 percent increase," which still only brought the annual salary up to $28,728.[11] Although Bellevue is a relatively affluent part of the state, with a median income of $94,638, those choosing to serve on the council have to be able to "afford" it.[12]

For parents with young children, childcare concerns function as an additional cost associated with public life. In 2017, Michigan state representative Stephanie Chang came under public scrutiny for bringing her toddler to a public meeting. A member of a community Facebook group posted the following:

> If you can't find someone to watch your kid among all your friends, relatives and hundreds of community contacts, stay home and don't disrupt a meeting for adults. If you take your kid with you when the legislature is in session, then there is something very wrong with state government.[13]

Although this kind of public and specific critique is not prevalent, more subtle critiques are pervasive, especially for women.

Rebecca Jimenez, who served as mayor of Guadalupe, Arizona, multiple times between 2007 and 2016, was charged a $10,000 fine and put on probation for receiving food stamps (officially known as Supplemental Nutrition Assistance Program benefits) from 2011 to 2013. Rebecca earned a $300 monthly salary as mayor, officially considered a part-time job but unofficially an all-consuming role. A mother of five, she didn't declare her husband's income on forms applying for assistance. Privately, Rebecca indicated that she and her husband were temporarily living apart and she needed the support. Publicly, this was unknown and unofficial, leading to an investigation into food stamp claims for which the family was ineligible if her husband's salary was considered part of their income.

Rebecca is no ordinary small-town mayor. She looks maternal, with a full face and generous build. Long black hair cascades down her back, and she is often dressed in bright colors. When she speaks about any injustice to the people of Guadalupe, or Arizona in general, her voice becomes defiant. Guadalupe is a small town of 6,000 people, nestled in Maricopa County, about ten minutes from the Phoenix airport. Its town motto is "Where three cultures flourish," a reference to the predominant Native American Yaqui tribe, Mexican communities, and farming culture.

When the anti–immigrant sheriff Joe Arpaio began his infamous sweeps in the county, he came face-to-face with Rebecca. In the parking lot of a Family Dollar store, she demanded that he end the sweeps in her town. Their standoff made national news in April of 2008, and is believed to have been one catalyst causing then mayor Phil Gordon of Phoenix to request federal investigations into the sheriff's activities.

The downward spiral from that fierce action to a conviction over falsely claiming food stamps is baffling. What would lead a public official to falsely access benefits in a small town? Not only did this create a public scandal and result in a conviction, but it also led to a recall election in which Rebecca was defeated by then council member Angie Perez in March of 2016. Rebecca has now withdrawn from public life, leaving her case open to interpretation. One perception is that this was a case of deliberate fraudulent activity by a public figure who never expected to get caught. Another perception is one that appreciates the private desperation that exists alongside public pressures to keep up appearances while holding an outwardly facing role in public office.

These are the invisible lives of American legislators. They are real people with real-life concerns, similar to those of most

Americans. When the public sees them, they see leaders whose passion, conviction, and courage is often motivated by their personal experiences as immigrants and refugees, as working-class students, or as LGBT or student rights advocates. They may have these experiences in common with other Americans, especially those who are also newcomers themselves, but their ascension to a public role places them on a pedestal for admiration and inspiration; they no longer look like peers struggling with mundane financial and administrative concerns. Voters respect them and want them to stay in office to advocate for their interests, but don't have a window into the hustling required to win elected office, get appointed, and fight for legislation. Often candidates themselves don't fully understand the financial challenges of being in office, since public perception of these roles tends to reflect success rather than struggle.

In places like Los Angeles, city councilors earn a generous yearly salary of $184,610, more than the governor, state legislators, and most members of Congress.[14] In New York City, council members make $148,500, less than the governor's $179,000 but more than state legislators at $79,500. Accompanied by headlines such as "NYC City Council Members Just Got a Huge Pay Raise" and "174 percent pay increase for LA school board," these outliers contribute to the public's perception that elected officials are living high on the hog.[15]

Often these high salaries go to elected officials in big cities, where the costs of living are higher and the sizes of the districts are larger, increasing the scope of a legislator's work, the number of hours spent in the role, and the level of complexity of the services they oversee.[16] For example, New York City council districts have approximately 150,000 residents, and Los Angeles 250,000 or so. In other cities, however, council districts have fewer than 20,000 residents, making them more easily governable by part-time legislators. But in general, salary differences are not clearly determined by any one factor, and what a local elected official might earn and how much time they spend on the job does influence who is able to run and serve.

For most ordinary people, the costs of entering and staying in public office are highly prohibitive. The number of zeros attached to campaigns seems to increase with each election cycle. Advocates for political reform are fighting for policies that can limit the amount spent on campaigns and make more transparent the so-called dark money that supports some candidates' campaigns for public office. At the national level, these groups include Represent.US and Every Voice. The former has chapters across the country working on anti-corruption measures that include disclosing political money online and introducing measures to give voters a credit they can use toward a political donation. Every Voice is singularly focused on increasing the number of small donors to elections and helps conceive and pass programs around the country.

What is missing from these conversations about money and politics are the financial safeguards needed to allow anyone— not just the wealthy—to choose public life and stay there. Even if an increasing number of cities and states implement programs that allow more voters or residents to support political campaigns, leaders who come from minority, immigrant, and low-income backgrounds will still struggle with having enough resources to consider running in the first place and to balance public life with personal financial concerns.

Candidates are often advised to have three to six months' worth of savings going into a campaign. Ideally, this cushion allows candidates to dedicate themselves full-time to a campaign in the final stretch, but of course, that's not always possible. Candidates also have to hold jobs in industries that will give them a leave of absence for their campaign, or feel confident that they can secure new jobs if the campaign doesn't work out. Even with job security, the debts incurred in campaigns can be prohibitive for many, particularly those having limited first-generation financial stability rather than family wealth.

First-time, working-class, and low-income candidates of color are less likely to quit their jobs, opting to continue earning for as long as they can. Often, they work all day at their full-time jobs and campaign on weekends and evenings. As Jessie experienced, this schedule doesn't stop once you're in office.

In fact, when newly elected, legislators' stress is exacerbated by the expectation that they be on a steep learning curve, and need to respond to bills on subjects as diverse as reproductive justice and campaign finance. They become at once experts on everything and experts on nothing. Because they are seen as people with power and resources, people like Jessie often go from being surrounded by community support to being lonely advocates in their legislatures.

How these newcomers make it into local and state legislatures, and whether they can stay in office, matters for the future of our democracy. Their voices bring perspectives to policymaking that reflect the needs of their constituents, many of whom share similar economic concerns. If rich white men are making most laws, those decisions are less likely to reflect the concerns of an economically and culturally diverse American public. The more alienated everyday voters feel from the decision-making process, the less likely they are to feel adequately represented. Decreased engagement and participation in turn hurts democracy.

Every public official faces sustained demands on her time, to fundraise, be in the community, and make policy. But if you're an everyday American, with the same working-class or middle-class struggles as your voters, you're more likely to bring these perspectives to bear on policymaking. And like the legislators discussed here, whose lives are shaped by the intersection of race, class, immigration status, sexual orientation, and religious beliefs, each of these experiences can be brought to bear on their work, not just one at a time but altogether.

To ensure that more people like Athena, Carmen, Jessie, Juan, and Rebecca are elected and continue to serve, legislators' salaries need to be adjusted to reflect cost-of-living increases over the last few decades. Salaries in Arizona and Colorado haven't been adjusted for nearly twenty years, not since 1999. The National Council on State Legislatures, a nonprofit that serves as a resource and advocate, has found that the average state legislator's salary has actually decreased over the past thirty years, if adjusted for inflation.[17]

Salary should not be a deterrent to running for public office, and once in office, legislators must be able to focus on their job serving their districts, rather than on worrying about how they can pick up additional work to help balance their financial needs. But the power to change salaries rests with the legislators themselves, which puts them in the awkward position of voting on their own raises.

They also need support to serve, with more and better-paid staff who can help with research, for example, to ensure that they have the adequate, unbiased information they need to make sound policy decisions. But professionalizing legislators' and staff salaries can prove unpopular with voters, who are themselves struggling to make ends meet.

One way to argue for salaries that adequately meet cost-of-living requirements and provide for adequate staffing levels is to focus on conflict-of-interest and ethical concerns. If a city council member is being paid by the city and also by a non-profit, her loyalties could be divided. If a legislator receives a salary from the state and runs a business, is it easier for him to solicit contracts from fellow legislators? If a legislator's office is understaffed and relies on reports generated by special interest groups to draft legislation, conflicts can arise about who is being served by a policy. These are arguments that can help shift public opinion to support more resources for legislators' salaries and staffing.

With greater occupational and income diversity, legislatures are more likely to change economic conditions and opportunities for everyone. Mostly male businesspeople and lawyers cannot reflect the reality of educators, social workers, or working mothers, for example. Those voices are needed at the policymaking table, both to introduce new perspectives to the conversation and to be a mirror to others in the community of who an American leader can be. Opening up the pathways to political office for newcomers is not just a nice thing to do; it is a critical step in connecting demographics to destiny, for those who run but also for those whom they represent.

6

IN IT TO WIN IT

The daughter of Cuban parents, Yvanna Cancela grew up in Florida and moved to Nevada soon after graduating from college, in pursuit of a unique element of the American dream—political engagement. The first American-born person in her family, Yvanna was appointed state senator for District 10 in 2016, just over six years after she first came to the Silver State. She hadn't planned for a career in political office, but, looking at the steps she took after college, her appointment seems almost preordained.

Yvanna hasn't left politics since that first foray. Tall and dark-haired, with an affinity for high heels, she talks quickly and with authority about the issues affecting her constituents and working people in Nevada. Her long hair is often pulled back in a ponytail, contributing to an air of no nonsense. But she is open and especially bubbly when she talks about finding a calling in politics, which happened almost coincidentally.

Originally intending to join the Peace Corps after college, Yvanna instead found her way to Nevada in 2010 to work on then senator Harry Reid's 2010 re-election campaign. She first met the former senator when she was a rising senior at Northwestern University; a friend sent her a notice that Senator Reid's office was seeking interns, and she applied. That experience not only introduced her to policymaking but also provided her with access to opportunities like standing on the balcony of the Supreme Court as associate justice Sonia Soto-mayor was sworn in on August 8, 2009.

After a summer doing bilingual outreach to the Spanish-language press on behalf of Senator Reid's office, she headed back to finish her senior year and plan for life beyond college. After graduation, unsure what to do next, Yvanna read that Senator Reid was down 20 points in the polls. She viewed him as a "titan of politics" and, motivated to join the campaign, de-cided to reach out to her former supervisor in the senator's of-fice. Through his referral, she connected to a campaign staffer in Nevada and was hired as a field organizer for Latinx out-reach. She headed out to Las Vegas in July of 2010, where she began knocking on doors and making phone calls to help the campaign reach its daily goals of connecting with Latinx vot-ers. Eventually, she also became responsible for recruiting and managing volunteers. Senator Reid's victory by 5 points over Republican challenger Sharron Angle has been explained by various factors, including overwhelming support by Latinx.[1]

After former senator Reid won, she went to work at the Cu-linary Workers Union, in part because on the campaign trail she had met D. Taylor, a formidable labor leader. He encour-aged her to think about organizing as a way to make change in the world, which appealed to her idealism. She started as a field organizer working with nonunionized workers at a local ca-sino and then went on to become a lobbyist. Just before her ap-pointment to the Nevada legislature, she served as the union's political director. In that role, she worked to ensure that union members, mostly comprised of hotel and restaurant workers, had an influence on the elections and policies that affected them. The union is a powerful force in Nevada politics because it represents workers in the service industries on which Las Vegas businesses are highly dependent.[2] In the last decade, it has also become a key mover of the Latinx vote, which has further bolstered its power and influence. Its 57,000 members are 56 percent Latinx and 55 percent women.[3] Yvanna's story may be different from theirs, but she is still tied by gender, ethnicity, and immigrant experience to the members.

Her appointment as a state senator wasn't the result of a traditional campaign, but was a turning point in her journey as a political activist and union organizer. Appointments can be a golden ticket for people like Yvanna, functioning as a way to catapult people into a position much more quickly and easily than they could attain it by running in a competitive election. Often, an appointment occurs when a sitting legislator runs for higher office or resigns because of relocation, corruption charges, or, as is increasingly the case since 2017, because of sexual harassment allegations. For those new to the political process or to the city or town in which they will run, securing an appointment can be difficult, but Yvanna was well positioned in 2016.

That year, Yvanna and her members juggled multiple electoral priorities. They were focused not only on the presidential race and the election to replace retiring Senator Reid, but also on the highly competitive congressional race for the 4th District, a new district created as a result of redistricting in 2012. The first person to go to Congress from that district was an African American Democrat, Steven Horsford, who had been serving in the Nevada State Senate since 2004. Two years later, Cresent Hardy, a Republican assemblyman who had been serving in the Nevada legislature since 2010, defeated Steven.

In 2016, the district was considered a battleground, or one that could be won by either party, because there was no established incumbent, the seat had flipped from one party to the other, and the residents were 30 percent Latinx. Seven Democrats competed in a primary to unseat the incumbent Republican. Among them was Ruben Kihuen. Ruben, like Arizona state representative Isela Blanc and Anaheim city council member Jose Moreno, had arrived in the United States from Mexico and was undocumented until passage of the 1986 Immigration Reform and Control Act. Ruben was elected to the Nevada State Assembly in 2006, when he was twenty-six years old, and then went on to serve as state senator. He represented the district in which Yvanna lived, state Senate District 10, which is 43 percent Latinx, 37 percent white, 11 percent black, 7 percent Asian American, and 3 percent multiracial or other.

Some politicians in Yvanna's network planted the seed early on that she would be the ideal person to fill Ruben's seat if he won his bid for Congress, given her political and community ties. One of them was Nevada state senator Tick Segerblom, an attorney who represents the third Senate district. Tick is an old-school liberal who Yvanna knew from her work as political director of the CWU. His suggestion didn't come as a complete surprise to her, but she felt encouraged to have the confidence of a senior politician.

When Ruben won in 2016, his seat was open for an appointment.[4] As it happens, Yvanna was at the right place at the right time to secure the appointment. Before the election, Yvanna had been planning to leave her job at the union and travel for a few months before returning to Nevada for law school in the fall of 2018. But the Hillary Clinton presidential victory she expected didn't happen. And like millions of other Americans, she was moved to take action. It took her forty-eight hours to decide she would apply for the vacancy.

The Clark County Commission, which represented Las Vegas and several smaller cities including North Las Vegas and Henderson, was charged with appointing Representative Kihuen's successor. Its seven members are each elected for four-year terms and represent the county's nearly one million residents by overseeing critical agencies, including water and medical services. They also oversee the application process for vacancies and appoint any necessary successor.

Yvanna not only filed an application but also worked hard behind the scenes to garner support. Her work at the union had laid a great foundation for key relationships, and she says it helped to have "people around you who are willing to open the doors that wouldn't otherwise be open to you." She called all the commission members and offered to meet with them individually, and she announced on social media that she was seeking the appointment. Both through her solicitation and the announcement, she got overwhelming support from friends, community, and union leaders alike. Community groups like the Latin Chamber of Commerce wrote in her support, as did unions within the building trades and service sector. Her own union colleagues and leadership strongly supported her application.

Only two other people had applied, and on the day of the vote, only one of those applicants showed up. Given her track record, Yvanna was unanimously elected to fill the vacant seat, making her the first Latina state senator in Nevada's history.[5] Her hard work had paid off.

Yvanna's political career evolved rapidly, a rare rate, especially for women and people of color. She thinks it has something to do with the city she lives in. Describing Las Vegas as "perhaps the last big American city where if you come with a vision, you can really make anything happen," she gushes about the opportunities she has had: to work with Senator Reid, have an impact on the state's politics through her union work, and now serve as a state senator. She also recognizes how uncommon it is for someone like her to have had these experiences, and that at least some of her rapid advancement can be traced back to Senator Reid, a powerful if waning force in Nevada politics.

Being a legislator in Nevada entails spending 120 days in session every other year. In between sessions, legislators research policy ideas and plan what issue areas they can work on when back in session. After Yvanna got appointed, she had two weeks to come up with issue areas and submit them to legislative staff to research and develop into potential bills. She submitted ten ideas, and eight of them were passed into law in the 2017 legislative session, including a bill regulating the cost of prescription drugs to treat diabetes. Yvanna understood how the legislature works from her time as a lobbyist and knew that passing legislation required successful coalitions of legislators, influential special interests, and real people. Her legislative success is a result of her political knowledge as much as her appointment was a result of her being active in political work and visible to leaders who make the decisions about who fills vacancies.

Each appointment process, for each seat in each state, varies. Often, one appointment can lead to another, creating a domino effect affecting several people, seats, and—ultimately—communities. Although the appointments process is theoretically quite open, meaning that anyone can apply, it favors those who have connections to the local political leaders and knowledge about how to leverage those relationships. As Yvanna was able to do in Nevada, potential appointees need to be skilled at running a "campaign" even though it is one that doesn't involve the voting public. Not everyone has job experience similar to Yvanna's that prepares them to do so. Sometimes, as in the case of Vandana Slatter, getting an appointment is a learn-as-you-go experience.

A Canadian immigrant of Indian origin, Vandana is now a state representative in Washington. She found her way there in 2017 through a domino effect that began when the state senator in her district was elected lieutenant governor. When she first decided to run for office, she had already been active on nonprofit boards, including NARAL Pro-Choice Washington. The governor had also appointed her to the state's Board of Pharmacy. The first time she appeared on the ballot was for the Bellevue City Council in 2013, in the city where she had worked and raised her family since 2003. Although she had felt the call to run for office for some time, she had waited until she and her family had the financial stability required to enable her to focus fully on public service. Despite her local roots and civic participation, she was not ready for the political games-manship that comes along with running even a nonpartisan race.

The local chapter of the Democratic Party is called the King County Democrats (KCD). They support candidates and legislation that affects the county, which includes the cit-ies of Seattle, Bellevue, and Renton, among others. The or-ganization is an important early endorser for races in Bellevue and other cities in their jurisdiction. Vandana hoped to secure their endorsement, but as a newcomer, she didn't fully appre-ciate its importance. When she filed to run for a seat on the council, in a public vote the KCD overturned the recommen-dation of their endorsement committee that they sole-endorse her, and instead chose to sole-endorse her opponent, Lynne Robinson. Among the reasons put forward for their decision was that Lynne was the "first to declare her candidacy," a fact meant to establish Lynne's enthusiasm but an unnecessary cri-terion for endorsements.

The election included a top-two primary in August, which allows multiple candidates to compete for one seat; the two top vote-getters move on to the general election. The long-term incumbent was eliminated in the primary, and Van-dana advanced to the general election against Lynne, a fellow

Democrat. Without the full support of her own party, Vandana accepted the support of the eliminated incumbent and three other council members who didn't identify as Democrats. She lost the race and felt the repercussions of accepting these endorsements.

In 2015, when she ran again—this time for an open seat on the council—she had the benefit of her 2013 experience, which she describes as "getting her political MBA." Knowing how important the King County Democrats' endorsement could be to her success, she ran a "campaign within a campaign" to win the support of the voting chairpersons of Democrats from the various legislative districts in King County. At the initial endorsement committee interview, the questioning signaled that she was still viewed as an outsider, prompting the chair of the Asia-Pacific Islander Caucus of the King County Democrats to step in and advocate for Vandana. He helped her prepare for the formal endorsement meeting, and Vandana called all the chairs and vice chairs of each legislative district organization, more than once, to ask for their support before the formal endorsement meeting and vote. This time she was successful, earning the sole endorsement of the KCD. She eliminated her Democratic opponent in the primary and won in the general election against her Republican-affiliated opponent by about 700 votes.

"The Democratic Party should be an even playing field," Vandana says. But her experience shows that relationships and networks can sometimes transcend determination, qualifications, and commitment.

After only a year on the city council, a new opportunity

opened up. The 2016 election had a domino effect on legislative vacancies. Pramila Jayapal, an Indian American activist
and Washington state senator, won her bid for the 7th Congressional district. That left a vacancy that was filled by the appointment of Rebecca Saldaña, an advocate who had worked
on a range of issues including immigrant and worker rights
and affordable housing. Vandana observed that this appointment process was highly competitive.

The practice of filling vacancies by appointment to the
Washington state legislature requires that precinct committee officers (PCOs) in the legislative district cast votes on behalf of those who have applied. PCOs are elected and serve as
party representatives, helping to ensure that local voters are
registered and informed about the voting process and Election
Day. For appointments, the PCOs send their rank-ordered
top-three nominees to the King County Council, a nonpartisan elected body that included six Democrats and three
Republicans in 2016. The council generally votes to approve
the PCOs' first choice.

In November 2016, Washington state senator Cyrus
Habib, an Iranian American who had served first in the house
and then in the senate, won his race for lieutenant governor of the state. His departure created a vacancy for the 48th
Senate district, which was filled by the appointment of state
representative Patty Kuderer, leaving her seat in the House
of Representatives vacant. This is where Vandana came in.
Community leaders, particularly women, approached Vandana and suggested she apply, in part because they wanted
a woman to replace Patty. She says it was the furthest thing

from her mind, and it took weeks of deliberation before she decided to apply. Despite the encouragement from those around her, she doubted her ability to navigate the appointment process yet again.

Early on in the appointment process, it seemed clear that the favored choice for the vacancy to fill the state house seat was Matt Isenhower. A Democrat, Matt had recently lost a tough campaign against Republican senator Andy Hill for the 45th Senate district. When the 48th district house seat became vacant, he moved into the district, and support lined up for him. By the time Vandana announced, another male candidate, Brayden Olson, a tech entrepreneur who was new to the district, had also applied. "Everybody was shocked when I threw my hat in the ring," mainly because she had waited to declare and because support had lined up for the two male applicants.

She quickly launched an intensive campaign for the appointment because she knew it would be hard to get the formal King County Council nomination if she didn't have the majority of the votes from PCOs. Informed by her experience running for the Bellevue council, she called and met with the PCOs individually, and simultaneously reached out to members of the King County Council, which had final say on the appointment.

"I didn't take anything for granted," she says.

Steady work and determination helped her line up PCO votes that put her neck and neck with Matt, who was the early first choice. A former "Obama for America" campaign volunteer helped her with a grassroots campaign to garner support from her fellow city councilmembers, while she focused on counting the PCO votes she would have going into the appointment meeting. As luck would have it, days before the appointment was due to take place, Matt withdrew unexpectedly for personal reasons; many of the votes he would have received went to Vandana. She quickly became the front-runner, winning 65 percent of the PCO votes and the unanimous approval of the King County Council.

Merely four years after her first run for elected office, Vandana went from being a political outsider to being a city councilmember in Bellevue, and then to being the state legislator representing a district that includes that city, parts of Redmond (where Microsoft's large campus is located), and the town of Medina (where Bill Gates lives). In those four years, she's been on the ballot three times, most recently in the special election for her House seat in 2017. Although she had no Republican opponent going into the 2017 general election, she had a Libertarian opponent, and worked candidate hours, campaigning in the off-hours she was not using to fulfill her responsibilities as an out-of-session legislator. In the latter role, she had to represent her multiple identities as an immigrant, woman, person of color, and tech-industry expert. All these perspectives inform the way she governs and speaks with her colleagues, but she is wary of focusing only on immigrant issues and is vigilant about ensuring that she is also utilizing her experience from the private sector and the tech world.

Once in office, candidates shift focus from their campaign to get elected or appointed to a strategy that brings issues to the forefront, moves a bill, or makes policy. As a woman of color, Vandana feels that her fellow legislators and constituents often look to her to lead or speak on issues that have a disproportionate impact on racial and ethnic minorities, such as the state's Voting Rights Act. But being an immigrant is only one aspect of new Americans' multifaceted identities, which go beyond gender and ethnicity. How they have been affected by their educational training, personal passions, and professional knowledge also inform their policymaking interests.

Vandana, for example, serves on the K–12 education, healthcare and wellness, and technology and economic development committees so she can use her expertise in the biotech and healthcare industries in which she worked for twenty years. As a co-chair of the newly formed science, technology, and innovation caucus, she also brings her enthusiasm and experience to bear on the committee's work. Vandana continues to remind her colleagues in "subtle and not-so-subtle" ways that she is a woman of color *and* an experienced healthcare professional, an immigrant *and* a former city councilmember. Recent legislation she has worked on reflects the range of her commitments: to help reduce the costs of prescription medicines, and to promote the use of electric and electric-hybrid aircraft for regional travel.

Like Abdullah Hammoud in Michigan and Ilhan Omar in Minnesota, Vandana wants to speak not just for one issue or community but for all the residents of her district. One-third of her district is foreign-born; 63 percent are white, and 25 percent are Asian American. The other 12 percent are African American, Latinx, or mixed race.[6] While Vandana's training in healthcare and her experience in the biotech industry inform her views, Yvanna's perspectives on policy are informed by the needs of the workers she worked closely with at the union. Both legislators bring experiences to bear on their legislative work that go beyond gender or ethnic identity.

They also bring to their work their experiences as new American women. When Vandana ran for re-election to the legislature, she won 77 percent of the vote in her 2017 primary. It was because she had built coalitions as a policymaker and candidate, garnering votes from all corners of her district and building relationships with fellow lawmakers. People told her she would win, that she didn't need to worry. But, she says, "I'm a woman of color in a political campaign, and I know I have to work extra hard to achieve my goals." Yvanna continues to be active in immigrant rights work and is the director of the Immigrant Workers Citizenship Project, a local nonprofit that helps immigrants to naturalize.

Maybe that's the upside of not being anointed with power easily—that new Americans and people of color work twice as hard to get elected and stay in office. In Vandana's case, the journey brought her to her desired destination, but she's still getting used to it. "I don't know what to do with success," she says, because it's been so hard to achieve. Yvanna is simultaneously in awe of and levelheaded about her role as state senator. She describes getting into public office as dependent on a "perfect storm of life stuff," but also knows that she wouldn't have been able to make as much progress as she did as a first-time legislator had she not had her lobbying experience.

Vandana's and Yvanna's appointment processes resulted in the selection of qualified and well-suited representatives, both of whom also had a track record in civic and political work. They strategically campaigned to key decision makers who would decide on the appointments, and intentionally focused on garnering coalitions of supporters from unions and community groups. They were in the right place at the right time, but, without their relationship-building and political savvy, they might not have been chosen. As newcomers, they're breathing new life into their respective offices. But to get there, they had to navigate the political status quo, winning over gatekeepers and party leaders.

Unlike Yvanna, who brought her experience and determination to the process, many others are appointed simply because they are insiders or fit the political needs of the moment. Who goes from being an outsider to being an incumbent is as much a function of the appointer's motives as it is of the appointee's character and qualifications.

Often the process of being appointed is unfamiliar until individuals become a part of a political network or are suddenly thrust into the process because of an opportunity created by a resignation or election. For newcomers, this is particularly problematic, as they are much less likely to know the power brokers, gatekeepers, and decision makers who help fill vacancies. Those familiar with the process, on the other hand, are sometimes reluctant to engage because it feels opportunistic and self-serving. The cycle of insider politics thus continues, rewarding those with the most access who in turn welcome others who have access.

Breaking such a self-perpetuating cycle requires that new Americans become more active in spheres that bring them into contact with political leaders. But it also necessitates more transparency from the representatives whom voters elect to make decisions about appointments. Communities who have been marginalized in political circles must encourage and support their young leaders to be well positioned for appointments or elections. Sending them to campaign trainings, encouraging them to attend local political events, and ensuring that current elected officials and party leaders are meeting with community leaders can all help place promising new Americans at the right place at the right time. Investment in a pipeline can lead to more leaders like Yvanna and Vandana, whose work positioned them to be the committed and qualified voices that are now helping to make policy. Over time, as more new Americans become the decision makers on appointments, they must be held accountable to be the *door-openers* to, rather than gatekeepers for, a multiracial and just democracy.

THE NEW WAVE OF LEADERS

Three decades before his historic election, Sam Park was born in Georgia Baptist Hospital. When he won his campaign for Georgia House District 101 against a well-liked moderate Republican opponent, Sam was widely celebrated for breaking new ground as the first Asian American Democrat to be elected in Georgia.[1] But in the months leading up to the election, Sam struggled to get support from his own party. His experience is not unusual in this regard. Even among Democrats, progressive newcomer candidates of color struggle to be accepted as viable and serious candidates.

Among the calculations that party leaders make are whether a candidate can raise money and mobilize a base of voters. These are of course legitimate questions, but they put nontraditional candidates at a disadvantage because they are neither well connected nor wealthy. They are unknown to party leaders and come from communities whose voting patterns are considered unfamiliar and unpredictable. Party leaders also consider a candidate's relationship to the party. For those new to the political process or to the city or town in which they will run, establishing these credentials can prove more difficult than for those born and raised locally.

Sam had compelling credentials but not enough of them

to be immediately embraced. Although he grew up in the county he now represents, he often experienced it as an outsider. His parents emigrated from Korea and settled in Atlanta in the 1980s. He attended a private Christian school, and as the only Korean American student there, he learned to "blend in." His father was an engineer at Coca-Cola before embarking on a series of unsuccessful business ventures. His mother taught piano and other afterschool classes. When Sam was eighteen, his parents divorced, and he helped his mother start a check-cashing business to keep the family afloat financially.

Sam moved quickly from college to law school, during which time internships that he held introduced him to political life. While in law school, he worked for the Georgia House, the Georgia Senate Democratic Caucus, and the Maryland state Senate, but he never imagined running for office. Like many first-time candidates, he describes himself as someone who prefers to be "behind the scenes." He waited until the last possible day he could before filing to run, and at that moment felt like he was "jumping off a cliff." What led Sam to overcome his reluctance to be in a public role?

In 2014, four months after the Affordable Care Act went into effect, then governor Nathan Deal blocked the expansion of Medicaid in Georgia. By signing a bill that put the decision to expand Medicaid into the hands of the Georgia General Assembly, the governor ensured that this crucial benefit would be subject to debate in a legislature not known to be friendly to low-income Georgians.

Later in 2014, Sam's mother, at sixty-six, was diagnosed

with Stage 4 colorectal cancer, which metastasized to envelop her entire liver; she was given six months to live. With the critical help of chemotherapy, her life could be extended by two years, doctors said. But because she didn't have private health insurance coverage, public health benefits such as Medicaid and Medicare were the only options available to her. The political became personal for Sam, and set his decision to run for office into motion.

Only thirty-one when he started serving in Georgia's legislature in 2017, Sam became one of the youngest legislators and the first openly gay man to be elected to the Georgia General Assembly. The district he represents is small, with 56,752 residents who are 13 percent Asian American, 42 percent white, 22 percent African American, and 18 percent Latinx.[2] It's nestled within Gwinnett County, which is the most ethnically diverse district in the southeastern United States. In 2010, the county became majority-minority, and by 2040, Latinx residents will outnumber whites.[3]

Sam had to overcome multiple outsider statuses: as a Democrat and LGBT candidate in the conservative deep South; in his working-class, Republican family; and as a challenger to an incumbent.

When he announced he would run, his family was shocked at his decision to leave his paid job as a lawyer to campaign full-time. He doesn't remember his family being particularly engaged or active in politics when he was a child. They voted as registered Republicans, mostly because as Christians in the South, being Republican seemed like an inevitability. Sam's early political affiliation followed the family path, until Barack

Obama was elected president. In 2008, Sam began a political transformation that led him to the Democratic Party.

Sam's family didn't understand the gravity of his decision to run until they came to his swearing-in ceremony. "When you come from working-class folks, it's hard to imagine yourself in these leadership positions," he has said about his family's reluctance to accept his life in public service. Other political newcomers like Detroit city councilmember Raquel Castañeda-López echo Sam's sentiment. For some parents from working-class backgrounds, seeing their children in elected office might feel empowering. But for others, protective instincts about their children's financial security and emotional well-being kick in when they hear their children talk about a life that will be both public and financially limiting. When candidates or their parents are immigrants, the desire to protect is also rooted in fear of being attacked as outsiders, concerns about family members' immigration status, or perceptions about government if they have come from nondemocratic countries.

Sam's sexual orientation also positions him on the margins of his family and church. He came out to his mother when he was in his early twenties, a process he describes as hard for her then, and now. Within the Korean American community, conservative values prevail, making it hard to be openly gay. Sam embodies the tension between these two identities. As a gay Korean American Baptist in the South, he learned to navigate many fault lines, a skill that ultimately benefited him when he ran for office. He understood the vulnerability that comes with being marginalized at school, within the church, and among his family, and it helped him to develop what he describes as "skin as thick as a rhino's hide."

Being thick-skinned was necessary on the campaign trail, where he worried that voters might make assumptions about him based on stereotypes. Overcoming such apprehension took time, and the journey didn't get any easier when he started knocking on doors. He campaigned primarily on the issue of healthcare, citing Georgia's poor record of insurance coverage. The state has the fifth largest uninsured population in the country.[4] On the campaign trail, no one expressed explicit concern about his Asian American background, but some slammed the door in his face when he introduced himself as a Democrat. Even presumably progressive voters from his own party expressed mixed feelings, liking him, but not feeling comfortable enough to vote for him because of his sexual orientation. Like other states in the South, Georgia has no laws protecting employees who are discriminated against based on their sexual orientation or gender identity. Views toward the LGBT community are generally less open in the South than across the country, and GLAAD, a leading national organization working on LGBTQ acceptance, indicates that Southerners are 5 to 6 points more likely than their national counterparts to experience discomfort at attending same-sex weddings or bringing children to those events.[5]

Sam had to deal not only with less than full acceptance from family and community members, but also with resistance from progressive groups and Democratic Party leaders, who could not see a path to victory for him in the district. Very few districts that voted Republican had "flipped" to vote for Democratic candidates, and nothing indicated that Sam's run would be an exception. Party and union leaders were also concerned about losing their relationships with incumbent Valerie Clark, a moderate Republican who had been support-ive of programs like the HOPE scholarship, which uses lot-tery funds to provide financial support to Georgia students attending public universities and colleges. Clark had lived in the district for thirty years and served as the principal of a local school. In the eyes of the existing political establishment, even though Sam was a Georgia native, he was still a newcomer: unpredictable and unfamiliar.

But Sam was undeterred. He had confidence in his ap-proach to voter outreach, one that was different than the approach Democrats had traditionally used. In Georgia, Democrats' traditional approach has been to focus on "flip-ping" Independents and moderate Republicans, and ignoring the emerging new American majority, which includes Afri-can Americans and also new citizens from immigrant com-munities. Although his opponent was well known and liked by more long-term residents of the district, new residents and voters didn't know or have any allegiance to her. That was Sam's window. Sam understood the demographic change in his district well before party leadership did.

Valerie Clark had received 10,492 votes in 2012, and had no opponent in the primary or general elections in 2014.[6] If Sam wanted to win, he only needed to get about 10,500 votes. He reached out to the almost equal percentage of Asian American, black, Latinx, and white voters in District 101; this multiracial group of Democrats formed his base. The campaign knocked on twenty thousand doors, 75 percent of which were opened by voters of color.

But it was his early fundraising success that eventually got him attention from the Democratic Party and progressive groups. He started with $1 when he filed, a poor match to the $50,000 his opponent had. But in the first quarter, he leveraged all his connections and quickly raised $15,000 from friends and family and put in $5,000 of his own money. For newcomer candidates, a strong showing in the first report they file about their fundraising sends a signal about the potential of their campaign. Key quarterly campaign deadlines coincide with the quarters in a calendar year: March 31, June 30, September 30, and December 31. Although Sam's opponent outraised him 3-to-1 over the entire campaign, getting off to a strong start brought him much-needed attention from the progressive organizations that work to elect Democrats. These include the Sierra Club, Georgia Equality, Planned Parenthood, and labor unions. The Democratic Party of Georgia also took note, especially since the highest amount raised in a different competitive district, House District 105, was a mere $10,000. A competitive district is one that is considered to be "flippable," or likely to vote for a candidate from a different party after historically being represented by one party.

Sam's persistence ultimately led to support from allies like the minority leader, Stacey Abrams, who is running for Georgia governor in 2018 and who helped Sam get one of his first political internships when he was in law school. He describes learning about the additional support that came via independent expenditures from progressive groups. "I didn't know what they were doing," he says, but in the final week of the campaign, "mailers flooded in" from these groups. As was the case in Jose Moreno's campaign for Anaheim's City Council in 2016 and Raquel Castañeda-López's 2017 re-election campaign for Detroit City Council, this practice is increasingly common following the 2010 *Citizens United* case. Groups use mailers to influence election outcomes for or against a candidate of choice. In addition to this hard-to-quantify support, Sam's campaign received contributions from Planned Parenthood of Georgia and several unions, including the AFL-CIO, the United Food and Commercial Workers Union, the Teamsters union, and the International Brotherhood of Electrical Workers.

It was a close race, and Sam won by a mere 1.5 percentage points. The victory was just outside the recall margin, which is set at one percent. A closer race would have led to a recount, or a runoff between the two opponents.[7] Because of how close it was, Sam expects his 2018 race, when he is up for re-election, to be highly competitive. Still, he swung the district by 8 points, winning 51 percent of the vote (compared to the 43 percent that Valerie's 2012 opponent had received), the largest increase for Democratic performance in Georgia in 2016. But he worries that Republicans will see his victory as an anomaly; in fact, Valerie returned to challenge him in 2018.

The legislature in which Sam serves is an outdated one. He describes being "transported fifty to sixty years back in time" when he goes to work. In part, this references those who are serving who don't reflect the current population of the state. Gwinnett County, which Sam represents, was 93 percent white twenty years ago. As of 2015, the population of 825,000 is 54 percent people of color, meaning white voters are no longer a majority.[8]

More broadly, the legislature doesn't reflect the state's demographics. While only 3 percent of legislators are millennial—born between 1980 and 2000—32 percent of the state's residents are. The state is 51 percent female, but only 23 percent of those serving in the legislature are. Until Sam was elected, only one Asian American, the Republican B. J. Pak, had served in the legislature (from 2011 to 2017), although 4 percent of the state's residents are Asian American.

As in other legislatures, and with elected officials like Athena Salman and Isela Blanc in Arizona, one challenge Sam faces is making a living while serving in office. An attorney, he currently supplements his annual $17,342 salary as a legislator by running a political consulting firm, which helps advise candidates on reaching voters of color.

Georgia's elected officials are unrepresentative of the state in part because the Asian American and Latinx populations are growing so rapidly. But not much is being done to harness those numbers for turnout or to create a pipeline of leaders who can run successfully for office. During his campaign, Sam was struck by the knowledge that the voter database showed more Democrats than Republicans. Here was demographic change and electoral potential that his own party had not kept up with.

Without his vision for his district and the role he could play, Sam would be just another elected official. But he understood the need for new voices to be represented in the rapidly changing state. He's committed not just to his seat but also to ensuring that Gwinnett County's elected officials reflect the new reality of their community—younger, and more diverse in class, race, gender, and sexual orientation. Sam, the candidate—representing everything that is bright and beautiful about a new America—was initially an anti-establishment candidate. In his case, the establishment included Democratic Party leadership and progressive organizations reluctant to rock the boat or unwilling to try new ways to engage more diverse voters. Now, in office, he faces opposition from a statewide Republican machine that is singularly focused on getting one of their own back in the seat, to hold on to its power, and, in the case of Georgia at the state level, its majority in the legislature.

The tables have turned so that Sam is now the incumbent, a hard-won fight. As a newcomer who is just developing relationships in the legislature and the community, he is different from long-term incumbents who have been in office for decades but don't represent the district's demographics, don't actively bring in resources to the district, and don't provide new policy solutions to the state capitol.

The desire among the political establishment to avoid the risks that come with newcomers is not unique to Sam's race, and it transcends political parties. Even in the most outwardly progressive cities like New York, outsider candidates face extreme obstacles. One obstacle is getting endorsements from unions, the Democratic Party, and the Working Families Party (WFP), a political organization fighting for an economy that works for all, which has grown in prominence in New York over the last two decades. These kinds of gatekeepers resist supporting candidates who are running against incumbents, even when those elected officials are poorly equipped to hold public office and fail to live up to progressive ideals. Gatekeepers in endorsing institutions and parties know·they can work in tandem with incumbents to create a symbiotic relationship. Incumbents benefit from financial support and volunteer power at election time, and gatekeepers benefit from keeping in power those they have access to.

Three years before Sam's election, Carlos Menchaca ran up against skeptical political gatekeepers when he ran for city council in New York City. Like Sam, he was widely celebrated when he won his race and became the first Mexican American elected to the New York City Council, but before winning he faced opposition from unions and fellow Democrats, who supported the incumbent he was challenging to represent District 38. The two men share a commitment to their Christian faith, which is often in tension with their identity as gay men. While Sam challenged a Republican who was generally liked, Carlos challenged a member of his own party.

A transplanted Texan, Carlos moved to New York City after graduating from college in San Francisco in 2004. He had applied to be a fellow with Coro, a national nonprofit leadership-development program with sites in five cities. The nine-month program gives fellows experience in business, nonprofits, and government, and Carlos was awarded one in New York. Following the fellowship, he worked in multiple roles in city government, and in 2012, he watched how

Hurricane Sandy affected poor communities in Brooklyn, with long-term, devastating consequences.

Hurricane Sandy barreled through the Caribbean and, on October 29, 2012, made landfall in New Jersey as a post-tropical cyclone. It caused a storm surge that damaged 350,000 homes in New Jersey and neighboring New York, shut down public transportation, resulted in long-term power outages, and became the second-costliest storm to occur in the United States since 1900 (the 2017 Hurricanes Harvey and Maria have now surpassed Sandy in damage).[9] Damage in New York City occurred along waterfront communities that are affluent, as in downtown Manhattan; middle class, as in parts of Staten Island and Long Island; and low-income, as in Red Hook. This last neighborhood is located on a peninsula in Brooklyn and is in Zone A, which is at the highest risk for flooding in a storm such as Sandy. Its lack of subway access had kept Red Hook relatively under the radar until the opening of Fairway, an upscale supermarket, and IKEA, the popular Scandinavian furniture store. A new crop of restaurants and ferry service from Manhattan brought more visitors to the area and made it more attractive to pioneering gentrifiers. But historically the neighborhood has been home to public housing and industrial sites.

Red Hook Houses, one of the largest public housing developments in the city, was one of the places hit hardest by Sandy. Weeks after the storm hit, residents were still living without power and heat.[10] Much of the response to support Red Hook came from volunteer and nonprofit groups, who provided food, blankets, and clean-up assistance.[11] First in his role as a representative of the city council Speaker's office, Carlos went to survey damage in Red Hook. Moved by the damage affecting residents and frustrated by the slow response from government, he immediately became swept up in the dire needs and the desperation of residents for basic shelter, warmth, and food. He describes those days as "Organizing 101: distributing supplies, getting information out."

Carlos was born in El Paso, Texas, one of seven siblings. Both of his parents were also born there, but his mother spent her childhood moving back and forth across the border to Juárez, Mexico. After she married Carlos's father, they raised their family in the city in which Carlos dreamed he would one day be mayor. When he moved to New York City, he initially felt like a country bumpkin. But his work and community experiences there ultimately made him a real New Yorker and perhaps have positioned him to fulfill his childhood dream of becoming mayor.

His first job after the Coro fellowship rewarded his interest in politics. In the office of then Brooklyn borough president Marty Markowitz, he had responsibility over infrastructure projects in the borough. Over the course of five years, he learned more about the borough, and the city it is nestled in, than many people who were born or lived there all their lives. Then, in 2010, City Council Speaker Christine Quinn, who was gearing up to run for mayor, hired him to be her liaison to the LGBT community.

Carlos describes that experience as a window into the contradictions inherent in that community, at least in New York City. He met some of the city's wealthiest LGBT individuals, while also working on the needs of the homeless youth in that population. Crisscrossing the city in this way gave him what he describes as "massive access," which no doubt helped him relate to a wide swath of voters when he ran for office. He has now run twice, first in 2013, in an insurgent campaign against an established incumbent, jumping in late to the race and inviting opposition from political insiders unlikely to support someone challenging an incumbent. His second campaign, in 2017, was a re-election bid that proved to be equally contentious.

That he won both races handily (59 percent to the incumbent's 41 percent in 2013; and 48 percent to his closest opponent's 33 percent in 2017) is a testament to Carlos's infectious commitment to public service and his stellar ability to pull together a broad coalition of support that engages multiple constituent groups—immigrant moms, long-term residents of the district, and progressives in the LGBT community, to name a few. His journey to a historic election in the biggest American city is a far cry from his early days in El Paso, where his siblings and mother—with whom he maintains a close relationship—are still based. In fact, in December of 2012, when Carlos was struggling with his decision to run for office after weeks of leadership and organizing precipitated by Hurricane Sandy, he went home to El Paso to be with his mother and siblings.

His assessment of that period of disaster response—of what he and others did to help serve and rebuild—also describes the shift in Carlos, from being a staffer working for an elected official to being a public leader himself. Unlike the sitting council member for the district, Carlos was present, showing up day after day and using his access to power brokers and resources across the city to help residents in need.

When Carlos decided to run, he committed an uncommon form of political heresy in New York City: challenging an incumbent from his own party. He also happened to be challenging a woman of color. Sara Gonzalez, a Puerto Rican who had served as a nonprofit executive, first got appointed to the council in 2002, in a special election to replace Angel Rodriguez. Council Member Rodriguez had been forced to resign after being charged with extortion.[12] After her appointment, Sara had run and won elections in 2005 and 2009 and was running for her last four-year term in 2013.

Sara's tenure on the council and relationships with fellow council members trumped her record of poor attendance at council meetings and low levels of legislative activity, even though Carlos was considered a dynamic and committed challenger.[13] A young male community organizer running against an established female candidate twice his age made this an old guard vs. new guard race.

At the time of his election, Carlos lived outside of the district he ended up representing. About six weeks after the hurricane, the first seed about running for the council seat was planted by a seasoned campaign consultant and former candidate who had observed Carlos's work and studied the district. Carlos understood instinctively that District 38 was made up of distinct villages—diverse residents of public housing, middle-class immigrants, and white hipsters, among others. When the consultant showed him how a victory could come from mobilizing ignored voters in each of these groups, his instinct was reinforced with a strategy. Despite this, his first reaction to being asked to run was "Hell, no." But the work around Sandy had awakened Carlos's latent passion for holding elected office. After a visit to El Paso to rest and be nourished by his family, he felt less conflicted. Amid maternal fears for his health and well-being, his mother ultimately lent her support and promised to travel to New York City for the election.

Things moved quickly after that. The formal announcement took place in February of 2013, approximately eight months before the primary. In New York City, Democratic voters dominate most council districts, meaning the results of the primary tend to determine the winner of the general election. In the case of District 38, the primary pit Carlos against sitting council member Sara Gonzalez.

The race leaned in Carlos's favor early on, when congresswoman Nydia Velázquez, the first Puerto Rican woman in Congress, who represents the 7th Congressional District of New York, endorsed him. She had some explaining to do, since her endorsement could have been seen as a betrayal to women and Puerto Ricans. But Carlos says she justified her endorsement by describing him as "someone who I know will fight for everybody in our community." She wanted a partner on the ground in the district, someone she could work with from her perch in Washington. That early bond with Carlos lasted, and a popular assumption among the New York political world is that she will anoint him as her successor when she retires (although she is just in her early sixties, and many Congress members continue to serve until their eighties).

The Democratic and Working Families parties dominate

New York City's political landscape. Although the WFP initially saw itself as an alternative to the Democratic machine, which helps anoint who will run and win in most parts of the city, the newer, once-brash entity has come to align itself with the Democrats in many races. Often aligning with the Democrats and WFP is 32BJ, the powerful local arm of the SEIU, the Service Employees International Union, which represents workers who clean and secure offices, apartment buildings, and schools. Other powerful unions include 1199SEIU, which represents healthcare workers; the Retail, Wholesale and Department Store Union (RWDSU); the Hotel Trades Council of the AFL-CIO, which represents hotel workers; and DC37, the public employees union.

In that first race for Council, Carlos and former council member Gonzalez split union endorsements, with many unions sticking with her as the incumbent. However, the RWDSU and the Hotel Trades Council supported Carlos in a desire to bring a more progressive voice to the council. The WFP wanted to influence the race for Speaker of the council, who serves as the head of the legislative branch, decides which council members get important committee assignments that are tied to resources, and helps determine which legislation goes before the council for a vote. The favored candidate for the WFP and among incumbent progressive council members was Melissa Mark-Viverito, who was a community and union organizer before she got elected to the council in 2006. A Puerto Rican, she had been elected from northern Manhattan in a district that includes East Harlem. The Speaker is formally elected by the council when a new term begins, and the race for Speaker involved ensuring that incumbent and incoming council members voted a certain way.

Carlos was one pawn in New York City's 2013 election chessboard. He happened to be a dynamic and effective pawn, serving the interests of 32BJ and the WFP, which wanted to have enough council members in place to support Melissa as the council's Speaker. In deciding to support his race, the union and the political party were lining up an additional vote in favor of their choice for Speaker. To some extent, Congresswoman Velázquez's endorsement was self-serving as well, as she knew it would help her secure an effective local partner, which she needed in order to adequately represent her district in Washington, DC.

Carlos says Nydia's early endorsement helped him go from nobody to being a viable candidate. But, in some ways, his entire professional life had prepared him to be a well-informed, committed crossover candidate who could relate and appeal to multiple groups of voters. Carlos could cross over from fellow Mexican Americans to other Latinx and immigrant groups, to white liberals and to the LGBT community. This kind of broad reach helps candidates like Carlos build strong, winning coalitions. It helped him overcome some resistance from within his ethnic community to win over the hearts and minds of his new constituents and the city's progressive power brokers.

He won the primary in 2013 by approximately 1,300 votes and promptly catapulted to national attention. He was celebrated as the first Mexican American city council member in New York City who was also openly gay and young (he was thirty-two at the time). And he lived up to his promise in his first term, bringing a municipal identification program to New York, to provide even people who are undocumented with government-issued IDs that allow them to access services. Although the program is attributed to mayor Bill de Blasio, Carlos authored the bill, introduced it with fellow council member Daniel Dromm, and shepherded its passage through the council. His district also broke a record in participatory budgeting (PB), a process which allows residents to influence how money is spent in the district. For four years, through 2017, District 38 had the highest number of participants in the PB process of any district in the city. Through this process, residents of the district—old and young, registered voter or not, citizen or not—voted on how the budget for the district was allocated. This afforded every resident an opportunity to have a say, regardless of their immigration status.

Even with these successes, Carlos had to fight hard to be reelected in 2017. Former council member Gonzalez came back to challenge him, but so did Chris Miao, a first-generation Chinese American lawyer, and Felix Ortiz, a sitting New York State assembly member who is Puerto Rican. This was an entirely different race than the one in 2013, with Carlos still representing the new guard even as an incumbent.

Felix Ortiz had served in the New York State Assembly for twenty-three years when he challenged Carlos, a move at least partly motivated by the much higher salary council members receive. Assembly members make $79,500 per year and travel to Albany for part of the year, a greater challenge for those who live in New York City, which is three hours away. By contrast, city council members make $148,500 per year and live in their districts year-round. But council members have term limits, and a recent trend has seen them move to state office, while state legislators move to city seats. This is a troubling pattern because it undermines term limits and serves as an additional obstacle for newcomers hoping to hold elected office. By running for state office from a perch as city council member, or vice versa, candidates are leveraging their position of power and established name recognition in the community, an advantage that candidates new to the community and to politics don't have. Rotation from one level of office to another means that the seats aren't as easily accessible to someone who isn't already in a position of elected power, and creates career politicians, whose primary experience is in public office rather than in the community.

Being an army veteran with long-term ties and loyalties in the community because of his incumbent status made Felix the most formidable challenger in the District 38 council race. The Policemen's Benevolent Association, which represents police officers; the teachers union, the United Federation of Teachers; and the powerful healthcare workers union 1199 all endorsed Felix. He came in a distant second in the primary, getting 33 percent of the vote to Carlos's 49 percent, which is a function of Carlos's track record, campaign strategy, and incumbent advantage.

Among New York City Latinx, Puerto Ricans have long held outsize political power, beginning in 1965 with the election of Herman Badillo, who served first as Bronx borough president and then in Congress. But since the 2000 census, the size of the Puerto Rican population has decreased and the number of Dominicans and Mexicans has increased. The Dominican community elected its own to office, beginning first with Guillermo Linares, elected to the city council in 1991. But until 2017, when Adriano Espaillat began his first term, the only Latinos in Congress from New York had been Puerto Ricans. As the city's Latinx population becomes increasingly multiethnic, tensions have emerged, such as those between Dominican and Puerto Rican leaders that surfaced during Representative Espaillat's first bid for Congress, against Charlie Rangel, in 2012.[14] But it's not just national origin that distinguishes candidates. Carlos also represents a "new school" of leaders who are more progressive. That can be threatening to current gatekeepers within political and business communities, whose self-interest may diverge from the economic needs of the city's working-class and immigrant communities, for whom Carlos is a strong advocate.

Newcomers like Carlos and Sam bring intersectional approaches—as gay men of color from working-class backgrounds—to their campaigns and governance, and more of them in office means more Americans are better represented. But these intersections threaten a status quo that prefers to rely on incumbents rather than to understand and engage new voters or to go beyond identity politics, a narrow perspective that assumes that one's identity—one's race, sexual orientation, or gender—is more important than anything else.

Sam and Carlos understood a new math that could bring them to victory. They looked beyond traditional calculations in their district and found a winning formula that included new residents and voters who didn't feel loyal to or cared for by the incumbent. Like Ilhan Omar, who defeated a forty-four-year incumbent in Minnesota in 2016, they saw that voters in their districts wanted someone whom they could connect to, not just on the basis of ethnicity but also on the candidates' understanding of their needs. The same issues that made Sam and Carlos decide to run were the ones they used to connect to voters—health coverage in Sam's case, and disaster response in Carlos's case. This approach transcended any single identity to lead them to victory.

Campaigns that suffer from myopic notions of representation and that focus simply on candidates' identities are shortsighted and out of touch with political realities. As communities of color and immigrant communities seek to build political power, intentional choices about candidates' views and policies must be considered alongside their ethnicities.

In 2016, the Latino Victory Project (LVP), a group focused on building Latinx political power, chose to endorse former California congresswoman Loretta Sanchez in her bid for the Senate. Loretta had been repeatedly accused of making Islamophobic and racist comments, and lacked the momentum of her opponent, Kamala Harris, another woman of color.[15] Both are Democrats, but Loretta won LVP's endorsement based on being Latina (but lost the race). Had the Latino Victory Project remained neutral in the race, even without citing concerns about Loretta's views or qualifications, they would have shown solidarity with other communities of color. Instead, aligning explicitly with Loretta sent the message that ethnicity mattered above all else.

A reflective democracy must mirror voters by ethnicity and gender as well as in perspective and experience. Carlos is as much an American and a New Yorker as he is anything else. Sam is a Southerner and Georgian, as well as being Korean American. What makes them viable is not just an ethnic identity, but their Americanness, embodied in a unique intersectional voice: LGBT working-class people of color. Any singular identity—ethnicity, class, or sexual orientation— cannot build electoral or policy coalitions. The work—and the victory—lies in creating a voter outreach plan that connects with a range of residents, a fundraising strategy that engages as many people as possible, and a policy conversation that brings multiple perspectives to the table.

Both Sam and Carlos had to overcome chasms in their districts, between Democrats and Republicans, anti-gay and LGBT-friendly, immigrant and not immigrant. On the surface, they represent the present and future promise of America, but underneath runs an age-old tension between those who have power and those who want to claim that power. For these two men, power is only worth having if it can be used to serve the people whose interests they have been entrusted to represent. Still, securing that power requires navigating systems and gatekeepers that tend not to be open to newcomers, regardless of their political persuasion.

Voices like Sam's and Carlos's are particularly welcome at a time when voters are dissatisfied with current political leaders. But people like them can't win in greater numbers without a reassessment of the same old strategies used to recruit candidates and decide who gets to run. Specifically, this entails gatekeepers being willing to lend support to incumbent challengers, especially those with the kind of authentic and inclusive approaches that Sam and Carlos took. The old formulas for determining a winning coalition must also be reexamined. Rather than relying on voters who have historically come to the polls, candidates and political consultants have to engage newly registered voters as well as voters of color who may feel marginalized from the democratic process because they have not been invited in. But most important of all, we need to expand the image of who an American leader is to include more people like Sam and Carlos, who can contribute to a seat-by-seat transformation of America's legislative bodies.

CONCLUSION: CORRECTING THE COURSE

These are times for despair and times for hope. On the one hand, immigrants and refugees are blatantly under attack as the Trump administration continues to press forward with policies like the Muslim ban, which "others" an entire religion and bars citizens of seven countries from entering the United States. Along with these types of administrative measures are individually driven activities such as the August 2017 rally in Charlottesville in which white supremacists led protests against the removal of Confederate statues. In contrast, and partially in response, progressive activism has surged. From protests at airports and court rulings against the ban to thousands of women and people of color signing up to run for office, optimism is high about a new wave of leaders and political activism. The 2018 election cycle offers excitement about the potential for historic winners and an increased number of progressives in Congress and legislatures across the country.

Thousands of first-time candidates are seeking seats on county committees and school boards, or vying to become mayors and congresspeople. Among potential historic races could be the elections of the country's first black female governor and the first Muslim women to Congress. It's a time to be hopeful, but also wary.

Missing from this fervor is a commitment to systems change that goes beyond individual successes to democracy reform, which would entail revamping the policies and processes that have kept people like us out of power. Structural changes that can help increase access to elected office by political newcomers will impact more than just first- and second-generation Americans. As the most marginalized groups in American politics, they need to be engaged as voters, donors, and candidates in order to make democracy more inclusive and representative. Their votes, voices, and vantage points matter more than they ever did before, for both demographic and democratic reasons. In numbers, they are a large proportion of the U.S. population. One in four Americans is an immigrant or a child of immigrants, and by 2040, that number will grow to one in three.[1] But voter participation among these groups is significantly lower than among native-born whites and African Americans. Fewer than 50 percent of eligible Asian Americans and Latinx voted in the 2016 elections, compared to 65 percent of whites and 60 percent of African Americans.[2]

Progressives lack a long-term strategy to leverage these demographics and to systematically and intentionally build power in legislatures. They hope that the new energy that arose after the 2016 elections will bring the right people into office, or, more appropriately, the right progressives into office, and better policies into effect. But without a plan that specifically identifies cities and states where intentional recruitment, policy work, and investment will occur, only a handful of the thousands of seeds being planted will bloom into flowers. Single victories are a start, but they are not a plan for long-term power-building toward a progressive agenda that serves the interests of working people and people of color. These everyday Americans are the ones hurting because of systemic white supremacy in our democracy, which affects who has power and for whose benefit that power is wielded.

The myths that have informed progressives' understanding of the political system are in particular need of an overhaul. One of these myths is that demographics is destiny. But Congress in the 21st century looks strikingly similar to the Congress of the 19th century. That's no coincidence. Changing the composition of Congress will likely take several election cycles. It will require addressing the structures that shape who gets elected, such as at-large elections and term limits. District elections create opportunities for political newcomers to run and win in their own communities. They have successfully created opportunities in California, Michigan, and Washington for Jose Moreno, Raquel Castañeda-López, and Carmen Méndez. These advances are not going unnoticed by opponents of democracy reform. The Project on Fair Representation filed a lawsuit against the State of California in 2017, challenging the state's Voting Rights Act on the basis that it allows race to be used in redistricting.[3] The lawsuit was filed by the same group that filed a complaint against provisions in the federal Voting Rights Act that require the federal government to approve changes to voting rights and procedures by certain states. That lawsuit led to the landmark *Shelby v. Holder* decision in 2013. In a 5–4 vote, the Supreme Court ruled that the formula used to determine which states needed pre-clearance was over forty years old and therefore outdated.

Moving from at-large to district elections is not just about race. It's about opening up the system to leaders who are valued and recognized in their communities, even if they don't have name recognition in the entire city. It creates opportunities for political newcomers to enter and win a race, despite limited political capital and resources. To ensure that our democratic destiny is in line with our demographic destiny, voters can learn from the experiences of the new Americans currently in office. One lesson is that single-member districts create unparalleled opportunities.

Other challenges in redistricting have to do with biased maps for congressional and state legislative districts.[4] Only twenty-one states in the country have commissions that are bipartisan or nonpartisan to help determine how these districts look. In other states, sitting legislators draw the maps of their own districts as well as their congressional colleagues' districts. The commissions have also been under attack, but in 2015, the Supreme Court ruled in *Arizona State Legislature v. Arizona Independent Redistricting Commission* that such commissions are constitutional. More states need to institute the practice of independent actors shaping the maps of legislators' districts in ways that are fair and representative to avoid cases like Pennsylvania's. In 2011, the Republican-controlled state legislature drew congressional districts that are believed to be among the most gerrymandered in the country.[5] As of February 2018, a protracted legal battle between the courts and the state legislature resulted in the Supreme Court imposing a new congressional map in advance of a May 15 primary. Although this opens up opportunities, the three-month window made it difficult for most candidates who are not already networked or resourced to run a competitive campaign.

Democracy reformers have work to do in advance of the 2020 census, after which states will be expected to redraw districts based on population changes. More states must revisit the rules by which districts are drawn. For Congress and state legislatures, these new districts may be the much-needed opening for communities to elect one of their own for the first time. If sitting legislators draw the new maps, they are less likely to create new opportunities and more likely to hold on to their own power.

But even with the advantage of districts that bring together communities of interest along racial, class, or geographic interests, money in politics can be an insurmountable barrier to newcomers. Public financing programs need to be more prevalent to help reduce the role of money in determining who has access to political power. *Citizens United* continues to be an overpowering force, but municipal efforts can boost the chances of newcomer candidates, as it did for Isela Blanc and Athena Salman in Arizona and Carlos Menchaca in New York City. While they may have to run against candidates who are not participating in clean-elections programs, they will at least have an opportunity to run. Without public financing, working-class people, immigrants and refugees, and people of color stand little chance of breaking into an exclusive club of the networked and resourced political elite.

These structural reforms are necessary to make elected office more accessible to political newcomers and therefore more representative and reflective of America. Immigrants and refugees, who bring layered experiences informed by gender, sexual orientation, religion, and class, are an essential ingredient to ensuring our democracy is truly of the people, for the people, and by the people.

In addition to dismantling the system that is rigged in favor of rich white men on both sides of the aisle, we must also shift the culture within politics about who can be an American leader. Ironically, voters are frustrated with the usual political insiders, but the system only works for insiders. Voters want authentic new voices but politics is designed to protect incumbency. New Americans can be those voices, but only if those who anoint and appoint are willing to change their preconceived notions of who can have access to power.

This shift requires a transition from identity politics to coalition politics, and from representational politics to intersectional politics. The case for new Americans to be recruited and supported for elected office might itself seem rooted in identity politics. But it is in fact a case for coalition and intersectional politics. Where identity politics is narrow and exclusive, coalition politics is broad and exclusive. While representational politics has tended to rely solely on one aspect of identity—gender, sexual orientation, ethnicity—intersectional politics engages and acknowledges multiple identities. Like Carlos Menchaca in New York City, or Vandana Slatter in Washington State, candidates bring their multifaceted identities to campaigning and governance to ensure that they reach all voters and serve all residents, not just immigrants, women, or the LGBT community in their district.

Coalition politics is at the heart of many successful

campaigns because, as a strategy, it relies on engaging voters from different communities and building a broad base of support that includes multiple allies and groups. A candidate elected by a coalition is also multiply accountable once in office. By being responsive to diverse groups of voters during and after election, she can transcend loyalty to one narrow group.

Intersectional politics similarly provides a wider lens from which to view representational politics, which is too limited a frame from which to build a more inclusive democracy. An intersectional approach acknowledges the multiple perspectives an individual brings to bear on decision-making, in campaigning, and in governance. How an immigrant who was the first in her family to go to college views tuition hikes is informed by her experiences as a woman, an immigrant, the daughter of low-wage workers, and a first-generation college student. In combination, these identities lend complexity and perspectives that help guide her as she considers proposed policies.

As America and its election districts become more multiracial, shifting the culture about identity politics is essential for inclusive democracy. Increasing political power among people of color threatens any status quo, not just rich white men's. In addition to existing tensions between whites and people of color, the dynamic between leaders of color can also be competitive, with different marginalized groups fighting to secure or maintain power. In the city council race for District 38 in New York, dynamics between Puerto Rican political leader Felix Ortiz and Carlos Menchaca, a young Mexican

American, represented tensions between the old guard and new leadership. In Michigan, similar tensions arose in the race for city council's District 6, as African American Tyrone Carter challenged incumbent Mexican American Raquel Castañeda-López with racially tinged rhetoric.

The new South will be a place to watch, as African American leaders conflict or ally with leaders from politically emergent groups like Arab Americans, Asian Americans, and Latinx. These dynamics are especially important to address, as racial minorities are often told that running for the same seat means they will "split the vote." This assessment demeans both voters and candidates, implying that neither can distinguish individuals beyond their visible markers of identity.

Identity is only one aspect of what might connect voters to a candidate. As American legislative districts become increasingly diverse, more candidates of color will run against each other, giving voters the opportunity to vote based on issues instead of ethnicity. Voters and candidates are multifaceted, and they bring all aspects of who they are to the ballot box, something political parties have been unable to understand, especially when it comes to women, people of color, immigrants, and refugees.

For this reason, new American candidates must not be relegated only to certain seats, or to majority-minority districts. Of the 435 congressional districts, only 123 are considered majority-minority, for example.[6] Rather than limit candidates of color and immigrant candidates by suggesting that they only have the potential to win in those districts, political leaders should embrace new Americans as the intersectional, multiracial coalition builders that they are. In the same way that white men can represent Arab Americans, Latinas can represent white men. This requires stepping out of old modes of identity politics to broader, more inclusive democracy building.

But that goal will be elusive as long as we see immigrants as not quite American, or as appealing only to a base of voters who look like they look. Intersectional politics is about a strategic and cultural shift that neither Democrats nor Republicans have yet begun. Voters are still grouped according to identity categories—Latinx, Asian American, white working-class male, soccer mom—that are overly simplified. Outreach tends to be less about issues and more about populating rooms with those who look and might vote alike. Reducing voters to constituent groups increases the danger of glossing over the multiple, and sometimes contradictory, perspectives that voters bring to their decision-making.

In general, progressives and party leaders have failed to invest in recruiting and supporting immigrant candidates to run and win in any election, rather than in just those contests in which the racial composition of the district is considered favorable to a particular racial minority. This exacerbates the political quandary facing our nation: outsiders want to change the status quo, and insiders need things to stay the same.

The best way forward is to recruit outside of the usual political circles, party leaders, precinct committee officers, and union leaders. Instead, the next generation of policymakers can come from community leaders, local business leaders, and teachers—"people like us," whose primary qualification is lived experience in their communities and shared struggles with their voter base. Recruiting in this way brings new players to the table, those who understand what policies are needed for their constituents. As Raquel Castañeda-López in Detroit, Athena Salman in Arizona, and Ilhan Omar in Minnesota have shown, people run for office for different reasons but they are most successful when they can relate to their voters and are passionate about responding to their needs.

Expanding our perspectives on who can lead us also requires that the progressive elite understand that money and politics is not just about the costs of campaigns and the role of corporate money in shaping the outcome of elections. It is much broader, and it penetrates every level of political life. Concerns about money serve to limit who can even consider running for office and whether they can stay there. Native-born Americans, particularly rich white males, tend to have the kinds of resources and networks that free them to make career decisions independent of financial considerations. Most immigrants, refugees, and working-class people lack these same resources and networks, without which it is much harder to seek and stay in political office. Changing who can serve requires creating new salary baselines and increasing per diem allowances, to make running and staying in office a viable career option.

In addition, legislators without professional, full-time staff are unable to supplement and contradict well-funded research, giving well-funded groups more power in the legislative chambers. Groups that lobby legislators also fall along a continuum of those with and those without resources. The best-resourced groups, who are not always working in the interest of the American public, are well positioned to present data and make their cases in influential ways.

Changing public opinion about the resources available to legislators—for their own salaries and for office and policy support—requires intentionality and commitment to update our democracy for the times. Once designed for land-owning white men, it must now embrace and work for a multiracial citizenry in order to be just and inclusive.

The challenges that political newcomers face are not just political, but also personal. As newcomers make decisions about running for office, they often lack support from their families. Sometimes, immigrants and refugees from non-democratic countries fear engagement with government. On a more personal level, parents are concerned that their adult children running for office will encounter public harassment and attacks about their gender or race. Although many parents help, even if reluctantly, on campaigns, candidates still grapple with feelings of unworthiness stemming from not seeing others like themselves in office. When they get elected, they can sometimes be the only person of color, woman, or foreign-born person in office. As the lonely voice on certain issues, they sometimes feel isolated and struggle with how to be effective when faced with opposition.

New American elected officials often feel like tokens when assigned only to committees on immigration or voting rights. This is as much a manifestation of identity politics as suggesting that a Latinx candidate can only run and win in a majority-Latinx district. Just as new Americans can run and win in any district in America, they can also work on any policy in America. Their perspectives are needed on every committee in every legislature, from the committees handling education to technology, from finance to affordable housing.

These microaggressions hurt more fundamentally than the political structures do, because they strike at personal vulnerabilities and feelings of inadequacy that are reinforced by systems and practices that marginalize people like us. This internal glass ceiling, and the external ceiling set by systemic barriers, require a cultural shift, one in which new voices are seen as the powerful heralds of the inclusive democracy of the future. The more of them there are, the more confidence they will inspire among future leaders.

A brave new American democracy requires grappling with these racial and political dynamics. At its core, politics is about power, and that will not change just because demographics change. To transform the conversation, the arena in which racial minorities are being allowed to play, or in which they have been comfortable playing thus far, must expand to include every town, city, and state.

The fear of this possibility has produced a "whitelash," or retaliation from whites, in the form of restricted access to democracy by voters and candidates of color. The Brennan Center, the nonpartisan law and policy institute working on democracy and justice, has identified twenty-three states around the country that instituted restrictions since 2010 that make it harder to vote. Working hand in hand with adoption of these restrictive voting policies is the use of biased practices and processes, such as the endorsement of establishment candidates even when qualified people of color are seeking a place at the table.

As the country becomes increasingly diverse, the struggle for power and leadership will increasingly expand to include more complex dynamics. Majority-minority districts designed to ensure that one ethnic group is more easily able to gain representation is a fix that will work, to a point. But as parts of the United States become more diverse, with multiple ethnic groups forming the local electorate, new alternatives will need to be explored. Garden Grove, California, is a city of just over 172,000 residents, and has a population that is 38 percent Asian American, 37 percent Latinx, and 21 percent white. New York City is similarly diverse, with a population that is 33 percent white, 26 percent Latinx, 25 percent black, and 13 percent Asian American. An increasing number of Americans identify as multiracial, making narrow identity politics even more outdated.[7] Rather than negotiating against one another for small pieces of the pie, racial minorities need to join forces to elect someone who adequately understands the needs of all groups.

A more inclusive democracy must be built on systems that can self-correct. Publicly financed campaigns, term limits, and district elections allow newcomers to enter politics as the local population changes to be browner or whiter, poorer or richer. With these systemic changes, newcomers can breathe new life into government, challenge machine politics, and thwart gatekeepers.

The political context in which these changes must take place includes new organizations mobilizing civic players and potential candidates, a changing labor landscape, and a leadership crisis within the two major political parties. In the organizational space, groups are tracking the Trump administration's activities, recruiting people to run for office, and publicizing meetings of city councils and other legislative bodies, just to name a few of the activities. Labor leaders, both nationally and locally, can help boost a candidate's chances at the polls, but they can also be guilty of preserving incumbent advantage at the expense of emerging leaders.

While the Republican Party is grappling with a leader who is alienating many of its members, the party has a clearer strategy for building a bench and recruiting more diverse leaders. Specifically, the Republican State Legislative Committee's (RSLC) Future Majority Project (FMP) aims to "identify, recruit, train and support candidates who better reflect the full diversity of our nation." The FMP invested $7 million in the 2015–16 election cycle to recruit and support Latinx and women candidates.[8]

The RSLC's counterpart, the Democratic Legislative Campaign Committee, has no comparable initiative. More broadly, Democrats face major divisions that stem from the 2016 presidential elections, when supporters of senator Bernie Sanders and former secretary of state Hillary Clinton clashed publicly and vocally, laying bare an ongoing fissure between insurgent and establishment forces within the party. In spring 2016, the Democratic National Committee elected former secretary of labor Tom Perez as its chair and Congress member Keith Ellison as vice chair. Both men bring diversity but no clear initiative to engage new Americans as voters or candidates. An inclusive democracy is not about checking boxes for gender, ethnicity, or sexual orientation; it requires a commitment to seeing and doings things differently, so it works for a larger cross section of Americans than is currently the case. Most importantly, inclusion requires a commitment to more people, period. Not just party leaders, not just incumbents, not just special interests, and not just current voters.

The new math that must inform democracy going forward must account for potential leaders, potential challengers, pressing interests, and potential voters. Who can be brought to the table to fill empty seats, to replace seat warmers, to revise the policy agenda? The answers to these questions lie both in established venues and in emerging arenas.

In both venues, we must seek out movement leaders— people who are motivated to lead by something greater than their individual ambition. Often, the spark behind this motivation is a transformative personal experience, like Sam Park's mother's cancer diagnosis, or the death of a sibling committed to community, as in Abdullah Hammoud's case. Other times it's the result of a frustration with the political status quo, as with Ilhan Omar or Jose Moreno. But each of them also had experience leading for a cause, whether in a union, a university, or a legislature. And those places are filled with others who can be recruited and supported for political leadership.

Colleges and universities are a good place to practice leadership, as students become newly aware of racial dynamics and class concerns in a larger arena than their home base. Tuition hikes, immigration battles, and curriculum content have all been the impetus for people like Athena Salman and Jessie

Ulibarri to organize and lead students. Those experiences set the stage for them, and for others, to run for office. Effective immediately, institutions of higher learning can do more to ensure that student leadership reflects the diverse experiences of their student body. That serves colleges in good stead now and builds a foundation of skills for future leaders from the new American majority.

Similarly, union members often go on to run, bringing with them perspectives about the lived experience of workers. As candidates, they can relate to their constituents and mobilize fellow union members. As electeds, and especially if they continue to work like Carmen Castillo in Providence did, they are bringing their daily experiences to the policy-making table. Given that two-thirds of union members are women and people of color, they are necessary soldiers in the democracy army.[9] While union members remain strong allies in democracy reform, union leaders are more likely to preserve incumbent advantage or be beholden to existing power brokers. That distinction needs to be watched closely.

Beyond unions and universities, new arenas from which leaders can be recruited and encouraged to run include movement spaces. Organic movements like Black Lives Matter are training grounds for socially conscious and committed people whose interests lie in systemic change. In addition, organizations that develop leadership qualities among people of color to organize, testify in government hearings, and speak publicly are important venues for developing skills and confidence. Most important, these are leaders emerging organically from the communities in which they live and work. No one is as invested as they are in their communities. No one is better positioned than they are to gain voters' trust and to engage voters who have never voted or rarely do so. No one is better informed than they are about the policies that can benefit their communities.

These movement leaders can not only benefit from systems change and culture shifts but, as they get elected and serve, they can also help build the inclusive democracy that invites more like them in. Younger, bolder, and more dynamic than today's members of Congress, they are of the people and for the people. They are the Americans who can repair our broken democracy and lead us into the future.

AFTERWORD

For nearly two decades, I was politically homeless. A citizen of Belize, I moved to the United States at the age of seventeen for college, and like other immigrants before me, I was seduced by the promise of America. I had been living in the United States for sixteen years before I could vote. In December 2000, I finally became a citizen in a moving ceremony packed with others like me: optimistic, grateful, and inspired by the greatest democracy in the world.

Becoming an American on paper is an often arduous and always bureaucratic journey that requires resources to pay application fees at different stages of the immigration process (for visas, green cards, and citizenship), studying for a test on American history that many native-born Americans have no obligation to take, and patience through a multi-year journey.

Throughout the process, although I couldn't vote, I was as civically engaged, if not more so, than my fellow Americans were. I started and ran South Asian Youth Action (SAYA!), a nonprofit to help young South Asians like myself integrate into New York City. In my role as executive director of SAYA!, I served on the board of the New York Immigration Coalition. On the coalition's advocacy days to meet with legislators representing the city, I shared the needs and concerns of the diverse immigrant communities in their districts. I did exit polling as a volunteer for the Asian American Legal Defense and Education Fund (AALDEF), helping to survey voters on their views after they voted on Election Day.

In the fall of 2001, finally eligible to vote, I had the opportunity to practice my newly earned right four times. I cast my first vote in New York City's primary election for mayor and city council minutes before terrorists attacked the World Trade Center. That day changed the course of many lives, including mine. My first vote didn't count because the primary elections were rescheduled, but my second one did. My third vote was in the runoff election for the Democratic mayoral candidates, and the fourth was in the general election that Michael R. Bloomberg won. In that election, voters also adopted a referendum that established an office of immigrant affairs in the city's charter. Six months after he was elected, Mayor Bloomberg appointed me the commissioner of the Mayor's Office of Immigrant Affairs. Had I not been a citizen, I wouldn't have been able to get that job.

Although the United States had been my home for nearly two decades prior to my appointment, citizenship cemented my formal relationship to this country and changed how I would see my work. Within days of my appointment, I was responding to inquiries from immigrant families I had worked with at SAYA! and from others around the city about their applications for citizenship or permanent residency. Many of these families had not heard from what was then called the Immigration and Naturalization Service (INS) for years.

They had missed weddings and funerals in their home countries because they couldn't, or were afraid to, travel while their paperwork was in process. Each situation was different, but the common threads were fear and confusion. Because I knew them, or looked like someone they knew, or had a name that seemed familiar, I became a point of entry into a system that was scary and inaccessible. Often, their applications had simply gone missing in a shuffle of bureaucracy.

Being a familiar face for people who were seeking to adjust their status was a relatively easy part of my job. Much harder was ensuring protections for those without legal status. During my tenure as commissioner, my office had to advise individuals who were affected by what was commonly known as Special Registration, or the National Security Entry-Exit Registration System (NSEERS), which mandated that non-citizen men over the age of sixteen who were nationals of twenty-five countries register with the INS. We also had to advise the mayor on how to handle the relationship between city employees (including local law enforcement officers) and federal immigration authorities.

At work, I was crafting policy recommendations that supported the needs of people who looked like my father, brothers, and cousins. At home, I was hearing heartbreaking stories from young people whose families I had worked with, and from my own family: bullied at school, targeted at airports, harassed on the streets. I was fortunate not to experience any major harassment personally, but I carried with me the pain of my community.

I served as commissioner for only two years, but I learned

the lessons that led me to start New American Leaders (NAL) in 2010—that familiarity and relationships with the immigrant experience brings something to policymaking that we can't teach, but can nurture. What if more people like me could decide how our schools, workplaces, and government agencies operate? What if more people like me could sit next to a legislator whose experience was radically different from ours but who, like us, valued opportunity and security for her family and community? NAL recruits and trains new Americans to run for local and state office, because we need to have a seat at the table in order to change the menu of policies that are on offer.

While I lived and worked in the United States, no one had thought to encourage me to apply for citizenship, and no one asked me for my vote once I became a citizen. In fact, it was years of self-motivated voting that led me to become a prime voter, one who is now called for donations and support regularly.

Every year, more than half a million new Americans gain citizenship. No one is working hard enough to bring us into democracy. Our commitment to and enthusiasm for America is a highly underutilized resource. We have fought and continue to fight to be at the center of a society that prefers us to be on the margins; to speak fiercely and loudly when we are asked to be silent; to step forward rather than to step back.

Not only are we not encouraged, we're often actively discouraged. Some of the applicants to our candidate training program have said:

As a young Latina I will immediately be underestimated as not being smart or capable enough to run.[1]

There is a strong push for people within the established party activities and I fear without those ties, I will not be able to find my way in.[2]

The largest barrier I can foresee is [not] having the skills needed to fundraise. This is one of the skills Latinos and working-class folks such as myself need to learn to compete against the economically privileged Anglo community who has access to more resources than us on average.[3]

I am concerned that I could be derailed by sexist, Islamophobic, and xenophobic vitriol especially if I run at the federal level.[4]

Different words. Same sentiments. We're not seen as leaders, we don't have the money it takes to run for office, and we're not connected to political power brokers. These summarize the thoughts and feelings of many immigrants and other people of color interested in running for office. Whether it's skin color, name, religion, or immigration status—or all four—some aspect of immigrant identity is or has been under attack as far back as the earliest years of immigration to the United States.

Nearly one hundred years ago, the Immigration Act of 1924 completely banned immigration from countries in Asia. The law also put annual quotas on the number of people allowed to emigrate from countries in Africa and southern and eastern Europe.⁵ During the Senate debate about this law, South Carolina senator Ellison DuRant Smith explicitly cited exclusion as its intent. "The time has arrived when we should shut the door." Explaining why, he said:

> I think we now have sufficient population in our country for us to shut the door and to breed up a pure, unadulterated American citizenship. I recognize that there is a dangerous lack of distinction between people of a certain nationality and the breed of the dog. Who is an American? Is he an immigrant from Italy? Is he an immigrant from Germany? If you were to go abroad and some one [sic] were to meet you and say, "I met a typical American," what would flash into your mind as a typical American, the typical representative of that new Nation? Would it be the son of an Italian immigrant, the son of a German immigrant, the son of any of the breeds from the Orient, the son of the denizens of Africa? We must not get our ethnological distinctions mixed up with out [sic] anthropological distinctions. It is the breed of the dog in which I am interested.⁶

Here is evidence of the racism that underlies America's immigration policy: the heart of the immigration debate, then and now, is about who a "typical" American is. Although labor market concerns came up as a rationale for the restrictions, the 1924 bill's explicit intent was "to preserve the ideal of U.S. homogeneity."⁷

Today, the immigration debate is informed by similar views. Republican congressman Steve King, from Iowa, tweeted in 2017 that "our civilization can't be restored with someone else's babies."[8] Donald Trump, in a widely reported 2018 meeting with members of Congress, referred to Haiti and countries in Africa as "shithole countries."[9] A permanent solution for DREAMers remains elusive, as Congress and the Trump administration continue to debate funding for a wall along the Mexican border, as well as the parameters of a policy that would provide a pathway to citizenship for some of the undocumented immigrants in the country.

The media, political, and social environments continue to portray and treat those who are not of "Anglo-Saxon" stock as second-class citizens. It's no surprise, then, that the majority of the first- and second-generation Americans who are interested in running for office are concerned about how their racial, religious, or ethnic backgrounds would affect their run for office.

When I founded New American Leaders in 2010, a wave of anti-immigrant legislation was sweeping through the states, including in Arizona, Colorado, and Kansas. And a big representation gap existed between who Americans are and who leads us. NAL's signature training, Ready to Lead®, offers ways to navigate the challenges and opportunities immigrant and refugee candidates might face in their campaigns. Entry to the training program is by application, which asks a series of demographic questions and requires essay answers to establish applicants' connections to immigrant communities, their perception of the barriers they face to running, and the ways in which they propose to navigate those barriers.

From 2011 to 2016, we had a total of 492 applicants. We

analyzed their responses and found that 295 applications cited one or more of these three concerns about running for office: race or other marker of "foreignness," potential challenges with fundraising, and lack of political networks or experience. The most common response was some marker of identity: skin color, name, accent, religion, or immigration status. Next was the concern that they lacked the financial resources needed to mount a successful campaign. The survey found that their unfamiliarity with the political process or connection to political leaders was of equal concern.

I know how they feel. I was one of them on that day in April 2002 when I joined city government, passionate but unsure, committed but under-resourced, and talented but underutilized. I learned on the job, as do many of us who join politics or government. NAL is a response to the disconnect between who Americans are and who our leaders are, between how we see ourselves and how we are seen, between the power we have a right to and the power we have.

In cities across the United States, NAL helps men and women unlearn the messages that are subtly and overtly conveyed to them when they walk into City Hall, watch television, or open the newspaper (or click on a news site). Invisibility is hard to bear, but being seen as inferior is a slow torture. If you're brown, an immigrant, a woman, a person of color, worship in a non-dominant religion, or queer—anything but a cisgender white male—when it comes to running for public office, you receive the message that you're not good enough.

This is the tension first- and second-generation Americans—and those perceived to be new even if they are seventh-generation Latinx in Colorado or fourth-generation Japanese American in California—must navigate. Making the decision to run often means sacrificing personal comfort for public service; for new Americans, the sacrifice is heightened because of their perceived otherness. They are already familiar with the bullying and harassment that comes from racism and xenophobia, but running for office makes it possible that this familiar pattern will play out in the public arena.

This book offered a glimpse into the stories and struggles of just a few current and former elected officials, a representative sample from the few whose names and victories are getting attention as a result of recent election cycles. In the long term, with the right reforms to our democracy, many more new Americans can run and win. In the short term, we have these exceptional journeys from which to draw inspiration for individual campaigns, policy reform, and culture change.

ACKNOWLEDGMENTS

Each of the "people like us" in this book trusted me with their hearts. They gave their time and stories to me freely and without expectation. I can only hope that putting their struggles and successes on paper is an eternal note of gratitude. Any weakness in the retelling is a shortcoming of mine, and for it, I ask their forgiveness. Abdullah, Athena, Carlos, Carmen, Ilhan, Isela, Jessie, Jose, Raquel, Sam, Vandana, Yvanna: you are all my extended immigrant family and you strengthen me by your example. Carmen Castillo, Lan Diep, Rebecca Jimenez, and Stephanie Chang appear in this book, and I am also thankful that I have met them and been inspired by their work.

Many other candidates and elected officials have shared their stories over the years, including Ghida Dagher, Rebecca Thompson, and others too many to name. Your names may not be in this book but know that you, too, have informed this work and helped it take shape.

Back in 2010, when I had the idea to start a program to train first- and second-generation Americans to run for office, many people thought I was crazy. But some cheered me on anyway. Foremost among them is Geri Mannion. I am forever grateful to her for believing in me and in the work I do. Along the way, Sarah Peter and Sue Van have joined the cheerleading squad. I am grateful to Geri, Sarah, and Sue for being confidants and advocates for my work.

My New American Leaders family—past and present, staff and board—have all been patient with me being out of the office, especially in 2017 and 2018. I am fortunate to work with the most committed people, and some of them especially must be named. Eddie Andujar, Marian Guerra, Jessica Lee, Eva Masadiego, and Carolyn Sauvage-Mar, for your enthusiasm and support in so many ways, *abrazos y gracias.*

For years, Nina Spensley, my co-conspirator in many incarnations and a kind of book doula, has encouraged me to write a book. This is not the one she expected; still, she supported it, read and commented on early drafts, and was the best cheerleader. Tyler Reny has worked with me at NAL and on this book, and I am deeply indebted to him for his thoughtfulness and thoroughness. His editorial and strategic input at a key stage in the manuscript, and his constant availability to fill in gaps, were invaluable. Thanks also to William Mo for providing timely and thorough research assistance, and to Sasha van Oldershausen, who did the same at an early stage.

I am grateful to Farai Chideya for connecting me to zakia henderson-brown at The New Press at a very early stage in this project. As my editor, zakia offered patient and detailed insight and analysis to make this book readable and coherent. I brought my inexperience and impatience with the publishing process to many of our conversations, and she gently brought me into line. Thanks, zakia, and the team at The New Press for your work on all aspects of the book.

Many people helped with earlier iterations. Gloria Totten and Brian Feldman—thanks for reading an early version and providing affirmation. Lynn Johnston, I am grateful for your skillful input. Thanks also to Frank Flaherty for his expert editorial guidance.

My friends are the best cheerleaders and critics. I am lucky to have many of them, but during this book process some were especially important. The biggest of girl power hugs to Aimee Allison, Chiqui Cartagena, Maria Hinojosa, Mitra Kalita, Annetta Seecharran, Andrea Shapiro Davis, and Rovika Rajkishun.

My family is everything. My parents Poonam and Vinod, without whom I would have no determination or ambition. My sister Komal, a friend and legal counsel. My brothers Heman and Dinesh, for their unconditional support. My in-laws, Gyaneshwar and Usha, for being patient with my constant unavailability.

Nothing would be possible without my husband, Anshu, and child, Yadna, who bring me unbridled happiness, shower me with support, and surround me with love. They suffer, not always silently, from my travel, writing, and community work, but they are always vocal in their pride and joy for me. I am enormously grateful to them for the morning coffee, evening cuddles, and everything in between.

NOTES

Unless otherwise indicated, all quotes are from the author's interviews.

Introduction

1. "Race and Ethnicity in the United States," Statistical Atlas, accessed February 23, 2018, statisticalatlas.com/United-States /Race-and-Ethnicity. Note that throughout the book, I use Asian American or the gender-neutral term Latinx except where Asian Pacific Islander American or Latino is used in an organization's name, in a direct quote, or in reference to specific individual whose gender is clearly identified.

2. "National Origin in the United States," Statistical Atlas, accessed February 23, 2018, statisticalatlas.com/United-States /National-Origin.

3. "New Census Bureau Report Analyzes U.S. Population Projections," United States Census Bureau, March 3, 2015, census.gov /newsroom/press-releases/2015/cb15-tps16.html.

4. Center for American Women and Politics, "Women of Color in Elective Office 2018," www.cawp.rutgers.edu/women-color -elective-office-2018.

5. Jennifer E. Manning, "Membership of the 115th Congress: A Profile," R44762, Congressional Research Service, January 17, 2018, fas.org/sgp/crs/misc/R44762.pdf.

6. "Do America's Elected Officials Represent Our Population?," Who Leads Us? Project, Reflective Democracy Campaign, accessed February 23, 2018, wholeads.us/electedofficials.

7. Christian Dyogi Phillips and Sayu Bhojwani, "States of Inclusion: New American Journeys to Elected Office," The New American Leaders Project, 2016, www.newamericanleaders.org/wp-content /uploads/2017/05/States-of-Inclusion-FINAL-12516.pdf.

8. "Modern Immigration Wave Brings 59 Million to U.S., Driving Population Growth and Change Through 2065," Pew Research Center, September 28, 2015, www.pewhispanic.org/2015/09/28/modern-immigration-wave-brings-59-million-to-u-s-driving-population-growth-and-change-through-2065.

9. "Chapter 2: Immigration's Impact on Past and Future U.S. Population Change," Pew Research Center, September 28, 2015, www.pewhispanic.org/2015/09/28/chapter-2-immigrations-impact-on-past-and-future-u-s-population-change.

10. Jie Zhong, Jeanne Batalova, and Jeffrey Hallock, "Frequently Requested Statistics on Immigrants and Immigration in the United States," Migration Policy Institute, February 8, 2018, www.migrationpolicy.org/article/frequently-requested-statistics-immigrants-and-immigration-united-states#Naturalization.

11. "Americans' Views on Money in Politics," *New York Times,* June 2, 2015.

12. National Institute on Money in State Politics, www.followthemoney.org/show-me?f-fc=2&c-exi=1&c-r-t=1&c-r-ot=H#%5B%7B1%7Cgro=y.

13. Money in State Politics.

14. "Dark Money Basics," OpenSecrets.org, The Center for Responsive Politics, www.opensecrets.org/dark-money/basics.

15. Chisun Lee, Katherine Valde, Benjamin T. Brickner, and Douglas Keith, "Secret Spending in the States," Brennan Center for Justice, NYU School of Law, June 26, 2016, www.brennancenter.org/publication/secret-spending-states#Introduction.

16. "Comparison of State Legislative Salaries," Ballotpedia, accessed February 23, 2018, ballotpedia.org/Comparison_of_state_legislative_salaries.

17. Christopher Ingraham, "America's Most Gerrymandered Congressional Districts," *Washington Post*, May 15, 2014.

18. Justin Levitt, "Where Are the Lines Drawn?," All About Redistricting, Loyola Law School, redistricting.lls.edu/where-state.php#communities.

19. "Race and Ethnicity in Yakima, Washington," Statistical Atlas, accessed February 23, 2018, statisticalatlas.com/place/Wash ington/Yakima/Race-and-Ethnicity.

20. "The Term-Limited States," National Conference of State Legislatures, March 13, 2015, www.ncsl.org/research/about-state -legislatures/chart-of-term-limits-states.aspx.

21. "Cities 101—Term Lenths [sic] and Limits," National League of Cities, December 14, 2016, www.nlc.org/resource/cities -101-term-lenths-and-limits.

22. National Institute on Money in State Politics, www.followthe money.org/show-me?s=CA&y=2016&c-exi=1&c-r-ot=H&d -et=3&d-ccg=12,15#%5B%7B1%7Cgro=d-eid.

23. Joel Kotkin, "The Improbable Demographics Behind Donald Trump's Shocking Presidential Victory," *Forbes*, November 9, 2016.

1: Redrawing the Lines of Power

1. Kristin D. Burnett, "Congressional Apportionment: 2010 Census Briefs," Report C2010BR-08, United States Department of Commerce, Economics and Statistics Administration, United States Census Bureau, November 2011, www.census.gov/prod /cen2010/briefs/c2010br-08.pdf.

2. New York lost 2 seats: ibid.

3. "Race and Ethnicity in Congressional District 6, New York," Statistical Atlas, accessed February 23, 2018, statistical atlas.com/congressional-district/New-York/District-6 /Race-and-Ethnicity.

4. Redrawn in 2010: "Census 2010: Gains and Losses in Congress," *New York Times*, accessed February 23, 2018, www.nytimes.com /interactive/2010/12/21/us/census-districts.html.

5. "Majority-Minority Districts," Ballotpedia, accessed February 23, 2018, ballotpedia.org/Majority-minority_districts.

6. Ballotpedia, "Majority-Minority Districts."

7. Yamiche Alcindor, "John Conyers to Leave Congress amid Harassment Claims," *New York Times*, December 5, 2017.

8. M.L. Elrick, "Is Detroit Councilwoman's Home Part of City's Blight Problem?," Fox 2 Detroit, September 19, 2017, www.fox2detroit.com/news/local-news/is-detroit-councilwomans-home-part-of-citys-blight-problem

9. "City of Yakima City Council District 2 Position Future Vacancy Application," Yakima City Council, www.yakimawa.gov/media/points-of-interest/wp-content/blogs.dir/2/files/sites/2/City-Council-Vacancy-Application-Form.pdf.

10. "Q & A: Montes Voting Rights Case," American Civil Liberties Union of Washington, accessed February 23, 2018, https://www.aclu-wa.org/q-montes-voting-rights-case.

11. "Race and Ethnicity in Yakima, Washington," Statistical Atlas, accessed February 23, 2018, statisticalatlas.com/place/Washington/Yakima/Race-and-Ethnicity.

12. "City Council Districts," City of Yakima, www.yakimawa.gov/council/city-council-districts.

13. More likely to be wealthy: Sean McElwee, "How to Reduce the Voting Gap," *Policyshop* (blog), Demos, October 30, 2014, www.demos.org/blog/10/30/14/how-reduce-voting-gap.

14. "Home page," Project on Fair Representation, www.projectonfairrepresentation.org.

15. J. Harry Jones, "Injunction Sought That Would Freeze Switch to Voting by District," *San Diego Union-Tribune*, www.sandiegouniontribune.com/communities/north-county/sd-no-cvra-injunction-20171023-story.html.

2: Waiting Your Turn

1. Author's interview.

2. "Ancestry in Minnesota House District 60B," Statistical Atlas, accessed February 24, 2018, statisticalatlas.com/state-lower-legislative-district/Minnesota/District-60B/Ancestry.

3. In the United States: Phillip Connor and Jens Manuel Krogstad, "5 Facts About the Global Somali Diaspora," Pew Research Center, June 1, 2016, www.pewresearch.org/fact -tank/2016/06/01/5-facts-about-the-global-somali-diaspora; in Minnesota: Benny Carlson and Stefanie Chambers, "A Tale of Twin Cities and Somalis Being Trumped," *MinnPost*, May 23, 2017, www.minnpost.com/community-voices/2017/05/tale -twin-cities-and-somalis-being-trumped.

4. "Ancestry in Cedar-Riverside, Minneapolis, Minnesota," Statistical Atlas, accessed February 23, 2018, statisticalatlas.com /neighborhood/Minnesota/Minneapolis/Cedar-Riverside /Ancestry.

5. Mayo Rao, "Rep. Phyllis Kahn, Rivals Heading to DFL Primary," *StarTribune*, April 10, 2016, www.startribune.com/dfl-caucus-to -decide-fate-of-minnesota-s-longest-serving-legislator /375132011/#1.

6. Mike Mullen, "Rep. Phyllis Kahn Says Ilhan Omar Gets 'Liberal, White Guilt-Trip' Voters," *CityPages*, June 24, 2016, www .citypages.com/news/rep-phyllis-kahn-says-ilhan-omar-gets -liberal-white-guilt-trip-voters-8381897.

7. Robert Stewart, "Rep. Phyllis Kahn Shamefully Disenfranchises Young Voters," *Star Tribune*, April 21, 2016, www.startribune .com/rep-phyllis-kahn-shamefully-disenfranchises-young-vot ers/376636071.

8. "Minnesota Women's Political Caucus," Vote Smart, votesmart. org/interest-group/763/minnesota-womens-political-caucus# .WmFWGpM-cUs.

9. According to year-end reports for the 2016 elections. Minnesota Campaign Finance Board, https://cfb.mn.gov/rptViewer/Main .php?do=viewPDF and https://cfb.mn.gov/rptViewer/Main.php ?do=viewPDF.

10. Eamon Whalen, "How Ilhan Omar Became the First Somali-American Muslim to Win Public Office," FADER, March 14, 2017, www.thefader.com/2017/03/14/ilhan-omar-first-somali -muslim-politician-interview.

11. 5,868 voters cast their ballots. In 2014, when Mohamud chal-
     lenged Representative Kahn, 4,281 votes were cast.

12. Reid Forgrave, "Ilhan Omar Wants to Make America Decent
     Again," *Mother Jones*, May/June 2017, www.motherjones.com
     /politics/2017/07/minnesota-ilhan-omar-muslim; Rozina Ali,
     "A Muslim Woman Also Got Elected Last Week," *New Yorker*,
     November 17, 2016.

13. "Results for State Representative District 60B," Office of the
     Minnesota Secretary of State, August 13, 2014, electionresults.
     sos.state.mn.us/Results/StateRepresentative/19?districtid=474;
     "Kahn, Phyllis L." entry, Minnesota Legislative Reference Li-
     brary: Legislators Past & Present, www.leg.state.mn.us/legdb
     /fulldetail?ID=10302.

14. "Race and Ethnicity in State House District 60B, Minnesota,"
     Statistical Atlas, accessed February 23, 2018, statisticalatlas
     .com/state-lower-legislative-district/Minnesota/District-60B
     /Race-and-Ethnicity.

15. "Fue Lee," Ballotpedia, ballotpedia.org/Fue_Lee.

16. "Race and Ethnicity in State House District 101, Georgia,"
     Statistical Atlas, accessed February 23, 2018, statisticalatlas
     .com/state-lower-legislative-district/Georgia/District-101
     /Race-and-Ethnicity.

17. Marian White, "The Top 10 Largest U.S. Cities by Popula-
     tion," Move, Inc., February 8, 2017, www.moving.com/tips
     /the-top-10-largest-us-cities-by-population.

18. "Race and Ethnicity in San Jose, California," Statistical Atlas,
     accessed February 23, 2018, statisticalatlas.com/place/California
     /San-Jose/Race-and-Ethnicity.

19. "Race and Ethnicity in Anaheim, California," Statistical Atlas,
     accessed February 23, 2018, statisticalatlas.com/place/California
     /Anaheim/Race-and-Ethnicity.

20. "Overview of State House District 26, Arizona," Statisti-
     cal Atlas, accessed February 23, 2018, statisticalatlas.com
     /state-lower-legislative-district/Arizona/District-26/Over
     view.

21. "Ancestry in State House District 15, Michigan," Statistical Atlas, accessed February 23, 2018, statisticalatlas.com /state-lower-legislative-district/Michigan/District-15/Ancestry.

22. "Section 1: A Demographic Portrait of Muslim Americans," Pew Research Center, August 30, 2011, www.people -press.org/2011/08/30/section-1-a-demographic-portrait-of -muslim-americans.

23. Dora Mekouar, "Are Arab Americans White? Maybe Not, According to US Census," *All About America* (blog), VOA, November 18, 2015, blogs.voanews.com/all-about-america/2015/11/18 /are-arab-americans-white-maybe-not-according-to-us-census.

24. "The U.S. Census," Arab American Institute, accessed February 23, 2018, www.aaiusa.org/census.

25. Hansi Lo Wang, "No Middle Eastern or North African Category on 2020 Census, Bureau Says," NPR, January 29, 2018, www .npr.org/2018/01/29/581541111/no-middle-eastern-or-north -african-category-on-2020-census-bureau-says.

26. David L. Good, "Orville Hubbard—The Ghost Who Still Haunts Dearborn," *Rearview Mirror* (blog), Detroit News, www.trimpe sculpture.com/press/OrvilleHubbard.htm.

27. Good, "Hubbard."

28. Niraj Warikoo, "Statue of Ex-Dearborn Mayor Orville Hubbard Taken Down," *Detroit Free Press*, September 29, 2015, www .freep.com/story/news/local/michigan/wayne/2015/09/29 /statue-ex-dearborn-mayor-hubbard-taken-down/73028440.

29. "Race and Ethnicity in Dearborn, Michigan," Statistical Atlas, accessed February 23, 2018, statisticalatlas.com/place/Michigan /Dearborn/Race-and-Ethnicity.

30. Free Press Editorial Board, "Free Press Endorsements in Legislative Primaries," *Detroit Free Press*, July 24, 2016, www.freep .com/story/opinion/editorials/2016/07/24/free-press-endorse ments-state-house-races/87461040.

31. National Institute on Money in State Politics, www.followthe money.org/show-me?c-t-eid=39849843#[{1|gro=c-t-sts.

32. cfb.mn.gov/rptViewer/Main.php?do=viewPDF.

33. Ibrahim Hirsi, "Minnesota Politicians Vow to Resist Trump's Executive Orders on Immigration," *MinnPost*, January, 26, 2017, www.minnpost.com/new-americans/2017/01/minnesota-poli ticians-vow-resist-trump-s-executive-orders-immigration.

34. Hassan Khalifeh, "A Day with Dearborn Rep. Abdullah Hammoud: A Young Arab American Strives for a More Welcoming Michigan," *Arab American News*, June 6, 2017, www .arabamericannews.com/2017/06/30/a-day-with-dearborn -rep-abdullah-hammoud-a-young-arab-american-strives-for-a -more-welcoming-michigan.

35. "HF 1576: Status in the House for the 90th Legislature (2017–2018)," Minnesota State Legislature: Minnesota House of Representatives, accessed February 23, 2018, www.revisor.mn.gov /bills/bill.php?f=HF1576&y=2017&ssn=0&b=house.

36. National Conference of State Legislatures, accessed February 23, 2018, www.ncsl.org/research/about-state-legislatures/who-we -elect-an-interactive-graphic.aspx#.

37. "The Term-Limited States," National Conference of State Legislatures, accessed February 23, 2018, www.ncsl.org/research /about-state-legislatures/chart-of-term-limits-states.aspx.

38. "Trump's Bureaucracy Is Nearly as White, Male, and Unequal as His Cabinet," *Quartz*, October 23, 2017, qz.com/1109087 /trumps-bureaucracy-is-heavily-white-and-male-like-his-cabinet.

39. Elise Viebeck and David Weigel, "Rep. John Conyers Jr. Resigns over Sexual Harassment Allegations After a Half-Century in Congress," *Washington Post*, December 5, 2017.

3: Hidden in Plain Sight

1. "Race and Ethnicity in Anaheim, California," Statistical Atlas, sta tisticalatlas.com/place/California/Anaheim/Race-and-Ethnicity.

2. "National Origin in Anaheim, California," Statistical Atlas, February 23, 2018, statisticalatlas.com/place/California/Anaheim /National-Origin.

3. Seema Metha, "Orange County Has Voted for the GOP in Every Presidential Election Since 1936. This Year, It Could Go Blue," *Los Angeles Times*, November 1, 2016.

4. Liam Stack, "Two Klan Leaders Are Charged in a North Carolina Stabbing," *New York Times*, December 7, 2016.

5. Muzaffar Chishti, Doris Meissner, and Claire Bergeron, "At Its 25th Anniversary, IRCA's Legacy Lives On," Migration Policy Institute, November 16, 2011, www.migrationpolicy.org/article /its-25th-anniversary-ircas-legacy-lives.

6. Chishti, Meissner, and Bergeron, "25th Anniversary."

7. Chishti, Meissner, and Bergeron, "25th Anniversary."

8. This body is now known as the Anaheim Elementary School District, after a 2016 name change. Art Marroquin, "Anaheim City School District to Be Clearer with Its Name," *Orange County Register*, March 10, 2016, www.ocregister.com/2016/03/10 /anaheim-city-school-district-to-be-clearer-with-its-name.

9. "History of Federal Voting Rights Laws," United States Department of Justice, www.justice.gov/crt/history-federal -voting-rights-laws.

10. Marguerite Mary Leoni and Christopher E. Skinnell, "The California Voting Rights Act," League of California Cities, www.cacities.org/getattachment/f736ba74-086a-4f5d-beb7 -853d898691d8/LR-Leoni-Skinnell-THE-CALIFORNIA -VOTING-RIGHTS-ACT.aspx.

11. Leoni and Skinnell, "Voting Rights Act."

12. Erika Aguilar, "Anaheim Voters Choose Single Member Districts," 89.3 KPCC, November 6, 2014, www.scpr.org /news/2014/11/06/47911/anaheim-voters-choose-single -member-districts.

13. Art Marroquin and Martin Wisckol, "Why Anaheim's Mayor Tom Tait Is Taking on Disney," *Orange County Register*, July 7, 2015, www.ocregister.com/2015/07/07/why-anaheims-mayor -tom-tait-is-taking-on-disney.

14. Linda N. Andal, "Public Hearing Second Reading on Ordinance Establishing Council Districts—Additional Cvap Estimates (2016

Acs Special Tabulation)," City Council Agenda Report, City of Anaheim, Office of the City Clerk, February 9, 2016, www.ana heim.net/DocumentCenter/View/11369.

15. Nick Gerda, Thy Vo, and David Washburn, "Disney Breaks Its Own Spending Record in This Year's Anaheim Council Election," *Voice of OC*, November 1, 2016, voiceofoc.org/2016/11 /disney-breaks-its-own-spending-record-in-anaheim-election.

16. Candidates' campaign disclosure statement, accessed on May 9, 2018, http://www.anaheim.net/2917/Elections.

17. "Citizens United v. Federal Election Commission," *SCOTUSblog*, SCOTUSblog.com, accessed February 23, 2018, www.scotus blog.com/case-files/cases/citizens-united-v-federal-election -commission.

18. Chisun Lee, Katherine Valde, Benjamin T. Brickner, and Douglas Keith, "Secret Spending in the States," Brennan Center for Justice, NYU School of Law, June 26, 2016, www.brennancenter .org/publication/secret-spending-states#Introduction.

19. Lee, Valde, Brickner, and Keith, "Secret Spending."

20. Gerda, Vo, and Washburn, "Disney."

21. Thy Vo, "Anaheim City Council Approves Massive Luxury Hotel Subsidy Deals," *Voice of OC*, July 13, 2016, voiceofoc .org/2016/07/anaheim-council-approves-massive-luxury-ho tel-subsidy-deals.

22. Matthew Cunningham, "Mayor Pro Tem Drama Ends with Moreno's Appointment," *Anaheim Blog*, January 17, 2018, www.anaheimblog.net/2018/01/17/mayor-pro-tem-drama -ends-with-morenos-appointment.

4: Dollars Make Sense

1. "Stoughton, Wisconsin—A Brief History," Wisconsin Historical Society, www.wisconsinhistory.org/Records/Article /CS2447.

2. Chishti, Meissner, and Bergeron, "25th Anniversary."

3. "U.S. Unauthorized Immigration Population Estimates," Pew Research Center, November 3, 2016, www.pewhispanic.org /interactives/unauthorized-immigrants.

4. Art Thomason, Jim Walsh, and John D'Anna, "Russell Pearce on Verge of Historic Loss in Recall," azcentral, November 8, 2011, archive.azcentral.com/community/mesa/articles/2011/11 /08/20111108russell-pearce-recall-trailing-jerry-lewis .html#ixzz1dDamALn0.

5. Thomason, Walsh, and D'Anna, "Russell Pearce."

6. "DoJ Adjusted Legislative District Plan, Metropolitan Phoenix Area," Arizona Independent Redistricting Commission, www.az redistricting.org/2001/Final/leg_doj_adjusted_11x17_phx.pdf.

7. "Final Legislative Districts—Approved 1/17/12—Maricopa County," www.azredistricting.org/Maps/Final-Maps/Legisla tive/Maps/Final%20Legislative%20Districts%20-%20Mari copa%208x11.pdf.

8. "Overview of State House District 26, Arizona," Statistical Atlas, accessed February 23, 2018, https://statisticalatlas.com /state-lower-legislative-district/Arizona/District-26/Overview.

9. "Terrorist Screening Center–FAQs," Federal Bureau of Investigation, accessed February 23, 2018, www.fbi.gov/file-repository /terrorist-screening-center-frequently-asked-questions.pdf/view.

10. "Individuals on the No Fly List Are Not Issued Boarding Passes," Transportation Security Administration, May 11, 2012, www.tsa.gov/blog/2012/05/11/individuals-no-fly-list-are -not-issued-boarding-passes.

11. "Terror Watch List Counter: A Million Plus," American Civil Liberties Union, accessed February 23, 2018, www.aclu.org /other/terror-watch-list-counter-million-plus.

12. "*Latif, et al. v. Lynch, et al.*—ACLU Challenge to Government No Fly List," American Civil Liberties Union, April 25, 2017, www.aclu.org/cases/latif-et-al-v-lynch-et-al-aclu-chal lenge-government-no-fly-list.

13. Max J. Rosenthal, "The NRA Isn't Changing Its Stance on the Terrorism Watchlist," *Mother Jones*, June 15, 2016,

www.motherjones.com/politics/2016/06/nra-isnt-changing
-its-stance-terrorism-watchlist.

14. Executive Office of the President, "Protecting the Nation from Foreign Terrorist Entry into the United States," *Federal Register*, February 1, 2017, www.federalregister.gov /documents/2017/02/01/2017-02281/protecting-the-nation -from-foreign-terrorist-entry-into-the-united-states.

15. Spencer Amdur, "Appeals Court Declares Third Muslim Ban Unconstitutional," American Civil Liberties Union, February 15, 2018, www.aclu.org/blog/immigrants-rights/appeals -court-declares-third-muslim-ban-unconstitutional.

16. "NOW: Arizona Refugee Leaders Are Criticizing President Trump's Executive Order on Resettlement," ABC15 Arizona, January 27, 2017, www.facebook.com/ABC15 /videos/10154449543011359.

17. Amy Howe, "S.B. 1070: In Plain English," *SCOTUSblog*, June 25, 2012, www.scotusblog.com/2012/06/s-b-1070-in -plain-english.

18. These numbers reflect 2018 requirements, slightly adjusted since 2016. Arizona Citizens Clean Elections Commission, www .azcleanelections.gov/en/candidates/running-for-office.

19. "First Look: Seattle's Democracy Voucher Program," Every Voice Center, honestelectionsseattle.org/2017-report.

20. "2016 Annual Report," Citizens Clean Elections Commission, February 23, 2017, www.azcleanelections.gov/File/306 /2016-Annual-Report.

21. "2010 Annual Report: Including a Summary of the 2010 Arizona Statewide & Legislative Elections," Citizens Clean Elections Commission, February 17, 2011, www.azcleanelections.gov /File/32/2010-Annual-Report.

22. Citizens Clean Elections Commission, http://www.azcleanelec tions.gov/en/resources.

23. "Political Nonprofits: Top Election Spenders," Center for Responsive Politics, accessed February 23, 2018, www.opensecrets .org/outsidespending/nonprof_elec.php?cycle=2010.

24. "Arizona Free Enterprise Club's Freedom Club PAC v. Bennett," *SCOTUSblog*, SCOTUSblog.com, www.scotusblog.com /case-files/cases/arizona-free-enterprise-clubs-freedom-club -pac-v-bennett.

25. Jeff Zeleny and Jim Rutenberg, "With a Signal to Donors, Obama Yields on 'Super PACs,' " *New York Times*, February 6, 2012.

26. These groups did endorse them in the general election.

27. "Race and Ethnicity in Tempe, Arizona," Statistical Atlas, accessed February 23, 2018, statisticalatlas.com/place/Arizona /Tempe/Race-and-Ethnicity; "Race and Ethnicity in Mesa, Arizona," Statistical Atlas, accessed February 23, 2018, statistical atlas.com/place/Arizona/Mesa/Race-and-Ethnicity.

5: The Costs of Public Life

1. "Providence, Rhode Island," City-Data, accessed February 23, 2018, www.city-data.com/city/Providence-Rhode-Island.html.

2. "The Three-Legged Stool," United States Department of Homeland Security, November 16, 2009, www.dhs.gov /blog/2009/11/16/three-legged-stool.

3. "Key Immigration Laws and Policy Developments Since 1986," Migration Policy Institute, March 2013, www.migrationpolicy .org/research/timeline-1986.

4. "Senate Bill 06-090," General Assembly of the State of Colorado, www.leg.state.co.us/clics2006a/csl.nsf/billcontainers/D44C4D 655410B398872570CB005DB438/$FILE/090_enr.pdf.

5. "Arizona's SB 1070," American Civil Liberties Union, www.aclu.org/issues/immigrants-rights/state-and-local-im migration-laws/arizonas-sb-1070.

6. U.S. Congress, *The Border Protection, Anti-terrorism, and Illegal Immigration Control Act of 2005 (H.R. 4437), passed by the 109th U.S. United States House of Representatives on December 16, 2005*, www.ncsl.org/research/immigration/summary-of-the-sensen brenner-immigration-bill.aspx.

7. "DPS by the Numbers," Denver Public Schools, accessed February 23, 2018, www.dpsk12.org/about-dps/facts-figures/#14 73890264817-1aa2ce27-4615.

8. "Race and Ethnicity in Adams County, Colorado," Statistical Atlas, accessed February 23, 2017, statisticalatlas.com/county /Colorado/Adams-County/Race-and-Ethnicity.

9. "From Thomas Jefferson to Arthur Campbell, 1 September 1797," Founders Online, founders.archives.gov/documents /Jefferson/01-29-02-0409

10. "Income, Poverty and Health Insurance Coverage in the United States: 2016," Release Number CB17-156, United States Census Bureau, September 12, 2017, www.census.gov/newsroom/press -releases/2017/income-povery.html.

11. Ryan Murray, "Commission Recommends 45 Percent Raise in Bellevue Council Salaries," *Bellevue Reporter*, December 20, 2016, bellevuereporter.com/news/commission -recommends-45-percent-raise-in-council-salaries.

12. "Bellevue, WA," Data USA, datausa.io/profile/geo/bellevue-wa.

13. Alysa Zavala-Offman, "A Michigan State Rep Dared to Bring Her Daughter to a Public Meeting and Some Dude Is Pissed," *Detroit Metro Times*, September 27, 2017, www.metrotimes.com/news -hits/archives/2017/09/27/a-michigan-state-rep-dared-to -bring-her-daughter-to-a-public-meeting-and-people-are-pissed.

14. The Times Editorial Board, "What Are L.A. City Council Members Doing to Earn Their Lavish Salaries?" *Los Angeles Times*, February 9, 2015.

15. Jen Kirby, "NYC City Council Members Just Got a Huge Pay Raise," *New York Magazine*, February 19, 2016, nymag.com /daily/intelligencer/2016/02/nyc-city-council-members-just -got-a-huge-raise.html; "174 Percent Pay Increase for LA School Board, Report Says," *Fox News*, July 10, 2017, www.foxnews .com/us/2017/07/11/174-percent-pay-increase-for-la-school -board-report-says.html.

16. "City Councils," National League of Cities, accessed February 23, 2018, www.nlc.org/city-councils.

17. "Legislative Compensation Overview," National Conference of State Legislatures, July 19, 2017, www.ncsl.org/re search/about-state-legislatures/the-legislative-pay-prob lem636360604.aspx.

6: In It to Win It

1. Arian Campo-Flores, "Did Hispanics Save Harry Reid?" *Newsweek*, November 3, 2010.
2. Dan Barry, "Latina Hotel Workers Harness Force of Labor and of Politics in Las Vegas," *New York Times*, November 5, 2016.
3. "Political Director UNITE HERE Culinary Workers Union, Local 226," UNITE HERE, accessed February 23, 2018, jobs .unitehere.org/job/13503.
4. Ruben has since been accused of sexual misconduct and has announced he will not seek re-election in 2018.
5. "Race and Ethnicity in State Senate District 10, Nevada," Statistical Atlas, accessed February 23, 2018, statisticalatlas .com/state-upper-legislative-district/Nevada/District-10 /Race-and-Ethnicity.
6. "Race and Ethnicity in State House District 48, Washington," Statistical Atlas, accessed February 23, 2018, statisticalatlas .com/state-lower-legislative-district/Washington/District-48 /Race-and-Ethnicity.

7: The New Wave of Leaders

1. He has since been joined by Bee Nguyen, who was elected in 2017.
2. "Race and Ethnicity in State House District 101, Georgia," Statistical Atlas, accessed February 23, 2018, statisticalatlas .com/state-lower-legislative-district/Georgia/District-101 /Race-and-Ethnicity.

3. Tyler Estep, "In 2040, Gwinnett Will Have More Hispanics Than Whites, Forecast Says," *Atlanta Journal-Constitution*, October 11, 2016, www.ajc.com/news/local/2040-gwinnett-will-have-more-hispanics-than-whites-forecast-says/aGgZpByhj8pGSAn86VkfpK.

4. Laura Harker, "Fast Facts on Georgia's Coverage Gap," Georgia Budget and Policy Institute, January 23, 2018, gbpi.org/2018/fast-facts-georgias-coverage-gap.

5. "LGBT Life in the South," GLAAD, www.glaad.org/southernstories/life.

6. "Valerie Clark," Ballotpedia, ballotpedia.org/Valerie_Clark.

7. "Georgia Recount Laws," CEIMN: Citizens for Election Integrity Minnesota, July 7, 2016, ceimn.org/ceimn-state-recount-laws-searchable-database/states/Georgia.

8. "Race and Ethnicity in Gwinnett County, Georgia," Statistical Atlas, accessed February 23, 2018, statisticalatlas.com/county/Georgia/Gwinnett-County/Race-and-Ethnicity.

9. New York City, "Sandy and Its Impacts," in *A Stronger, More Resilient New York*, 2013, p. 10–18, www.nyc.gov/html/sirr/downloads/pdf/final_report/Ch_1_SandyImpacts_FINAL_singles.pdf.

10. Lucas Cavner, "For Public Housing Residents After Sandy, 'A Slow-Motion Katrina,'" *Huffington Post*, November 9, 2012.

11. Tony Karon, "In Hurricane-Battered Red Hook, Disaster Is Breeding Resilience," *Time*, November 12, 2012.

12. William K. Rashbaum, "Brooklyn Councilman Is Charged in an Extortion Scheme," *New York Times*, March 29, 2002.

13. Reuven Blau, "Fight Over Red Hook Council Seat Pits Incumbent with Party Support Against Upstart Community Organizer," *Daily News* (New York), May 5, 2013, www.nydailynews.com/new-york/brooklyn/red-hook-primed-red-hot-fight-city-council-seat-article-1.1334488.

14. Ed Morales, "The Changing Face of Latino Politics in New York," *NACLA*, December 19, 2013, nacla.org/article/changing-face-latino-politics-new-york.

15. Phil Willon, "Rep. Loretta Sanchez Responds to Criticism over Comment on Muslims," *Los Angeles Times*, December 11, 2015;

Phil Willon and Jazmine Ulloa, "Rep. Loretta Sanchez Implies Obama Endorsed Senate Rival Because They Are Both Black," *Los Angeles Times*, July 22, 2016.

Conclusion: Correcting the Course

1. "First- and Second-Generation Share of the Population to Reach Record High in 2065," Pew Research Center, September 23, 2015, www.pewhispanic.org/2015/09/28/modern-im migration-wave-brings-59-million-to-u-s-driving-pop ulation-growth-and-change-through-2065/ph_2015 -09-28_immigration-through-2065-11.
2. "Black Voter Turnout Fell in 2016, Even as a Record Number of Americans Cast Ballots," Pew Research Center, May 12, 2017, www.pewresearch.org/fact-tank/2017/05/12/black-voter-turn out-fell-in-2016-even-as-a-record-number-of-americans-cast -ballots.
3. Steven Rosenfeld, "Right-Wing Group Seeks to Slash Number of Elected Minorities," *Salon*, October 13, 2017, www.salon .com/2017/10/13/right-wing-project-may-slash-number-of -elected-minorities_partner.
4. "State-by-State Redistricting Procedures," Ballotpedia, accessed February 23, 2018, ballotpedia.org/State-by-state_re districting_procedures.
5. Jonathan Lai, "Why Pa. Sends Too Many Republicans to Washington—and Why That Could Change," *The Philadelphia Inquirer*, August 14, 2017.
6. Ballotpedia, "Majority-Minority Districts."
7. "Multiracial in America," Pew Research Center, June 11, 2015, www.pewsocialtrends.org/2015/06/11/multiracial-in-am erica.
8. "Future Majority Project," Republican State Leadership Committee, rslc.gop/about_rslc/fmp.

9. Josh Bivens, Lora Engdahl, Elise Gould, Teresa Kroeger, Celine McNicholas, Lawrence Mishel, Zane Mokhiber, Heidi Shierholz, Marni von Wilpert, Valerie Wilson, and Ben Zipperer, "How Today's Unions Help Working People," Economic Policy Institute, August 24, 2017, www.epi.org/publication/how-todays-unions -help-working-people-giving-workers-the-power-to-improve -their-jobs-and-unrig-the-economy/#_note5.

Afterword

1. Joseline Mata.
2. Amanda Farias.
3. Gilbert Romero.
4. Sameena Mustafa.
5. "The Immigration Act of 1924 (The Johnson-Reed Act)," Office of the Historian, Bureau of Public Affairs, United States Department of State, history.state.gov/milestones/1921-1936/immigration-act.
6. " 'Shut the Door': A Senator Speaks for Immigration Restriction," History Matters, February 24, 2018, historymatters.gmu .edu/d/5080.
7. Labor market concerns: Faye Hipsman and Doris Meissner, "Immigration in the United States: New Economic, Social, Political Landscapes with Legislative Reform on the Horizon," Migration Policy Institute, April 16, 2013, migrationpolicy.org/article/immi gration-united-states-new-economic-social-political-landscapes -legislative-reform; preserving homogeneity: "The Immigration Act of 1924 (The Johnson-Reed Act)," Office of the Historian, Bureau of Public Affairs, United States Department of State, his- tory.state.gov/milestones/1921-1936/immigration-act.
8. Philip Bump, "Rep. Steve King Warns That 'Our Civilization' Can't Be Restored with 'Somebody Else's Babies,' " *Washington Post*, March 12, 2017.
9. Josh Dawsey, "Trump Derides Protections for Immigrants from 'Shithole' Countries," *Washington Post*, January 12, 2018.

INDEX

ABOUT THE AUTHOR

Sayu Bhojwani is the founder and president of New American Leaders, the only national organization focused on preparing immigrant leaders to run for public office at the local and state levels. She served as New York City's first commissioner of immigrant affairs and lives in New York.

PUBLISHING IN THE PUBLIC INTEREST

Thank you for reading this book published by The New Press. The New Press is a nonprofit, public interest publisher. New Press books and authors play a crucial role in sparking conversations about the key political and social issues of our day.

We hope you enjoyed this book and that you will stay in touch with The New Press. Here are a few ways to stay up to date with our books, events, and the issues we cover:

- Sign up at www.thenewpress.com/subscribe to receive updates on New Press authors and issues and to be notified about local events
- Like us on Facebook: www.facebook.com/newpressbooks
- Follow us on Twitter: www.twitter.com/thenewpress

Please consider buying New Press books for yourself; for friends and family; or to donate to schools, libraries, community centers, prison libraries, and other organizations involved with the issues our authors write about.

The New Press is a 501(c)(3) nonprofit organization. You can also support our work with a tax-deductible gift by visiting www.thenewpress.com/donate.